WHEN JESUS SHOWS UP

WHEN JESUS SHOWS UP

DR. JOHN BOEDEKER

XULON PRESS

Xulon Press
2301 Lucien Way #415
Maitland, FL 32751
407.339.4217
www.xulonpress.com

© 2019 by DR. JOHN BOEDEKER

All rights reserved solely by the author. The author guarantees all contents are original and do not infringe upon the legal rights of any other person or work. No part of this book may be reproduced in any form without the permission of the author. The views expressed in this book are not necessarily those of the publisher.

Unless otherwise indicated, Scripture quotations taken from NIV Scripture quotations taken from the Holy Bible, New International Version (NIV). Copyright © 1973, 1978, 1984, 2011 by Biblica, Inc.™. Used by permission. All rights reserved.

Printed in the United States of America.

ISBN-13: 978-1-54564-857-5

The Book Cover

The book cover was beautifully designed by Stephen Gifford. I want to honor his willingness to take on this project. He is one of the stories of transformation listed in this book. I communicated with him that I wanted a cover that would show the majesty and glory of God in Jesus Christ. One of the ways I knew God was in this book project was how Steve, in some supernatural way, knew what I wanted even though I couldn't express it very well. I believe that when people see this book cover, they won't be able to resist looking through the book. Thank you Steve for using your wonderful gifts to bless many people including this author!

The Author's Notes

- All scriptures in this book are from the New International Version, Copyright 1973, 1978, 1984.

- Not all names contained in this book are authentic. When such a name is used, it will have an asterisk (*) behind it. This is to protect people in sensitive areas who are under much persecution.

- It is our belief and trust that every story in this book is accurate and every person mentioned is an actual person. Much of this book relies on the memory of Judy and me. Where our memories have failed in any way, we are sorry. Thank you for your patience and mercy.

Contents

The Book Cover v
The Author's Notes vii
Preface xi
Introduction xv

Chapter 1: The Pursuit. 1
Chapter 2: Coming Home 10
Chapter 3: New Life Changes Everything. 16
Chapter 4: The Clash of Two Worlds 25
Chapter 5: The Call 34
Chapter 6: The Beloved Mentor. 45
Chapter 7: The Scholar and the Gospel 54
Chapter 8: Battle with the Mafia 59
Chapter 9: Cowboy Boots and the Gospel. 73
Chapter 10: The Korean Story. 94
Chapter 11: Ft. Lauderdale or Bust. 101
Chapter 12: The Girls at Hope Hill 124
Chapter 13: The Kendall Intervention 133
Chapter 14: Confessions of a Prayer Junkie. 147
Chapter 15: A God-Sized Vision 162
Chapter 16: Legacy in India and the World. 176

"Be joyful always: pray continually; give thanks in all circumstances, for this is God's will for you in Christ Jesus."
I Thessalonians 5:16-18

Preface

Why does one write an autobiography? It certainly can be ego driven and vanity motivated. Instead, I am hopeful that these are not the reasons for this book. I would like to think that this book will bring glory and honor to Jesus Christ who is the source of all that is really exciting in this life. When my wife, Judy, was in her late 20's and I was in my early 30'S, there was a mysterious invasion into our lives that changed everything. It changed our vocation, our destiny, our lifestyle and our family. This book is about what happened to us, who was responsible for it, why our lives changed so much and is written as a legacy to my wonderful family and my friends who have been on this journey with us. It is also writtten to those who read this book so that you may have your life enriched and your faith increased.

One of my hardest decisions was to write about my journey without giving full disclosure to the path that Judy has walked with me. I felt if we were both to write the book, we would exhaust our readers. I will say that Judy and I are so much "one" that not one event mentioned in this book was experienced apart from the wonderful support and/or influence of my wife. Judy will be mentioned at times because she has been an integral part of this story. Even as I write this, I have a dislocated shoulder gained in a spirited game of whiffle ball with my grandchildren. It may require surgery. As always, my wife was there in the emergency room, in our home nursing me back to health, in serving many ways to make my life easier and more productive for the Lord. She has been very involved proofing my writing.

This book could not have happened without Martie Tracy, who has been so helpful as an editor and educator. Steve Gifford produced the cover for the book and was able to capture what I was seeing, refining it and improving it with his incredible talent. Gary Shepherd gave me help on knowing how to publish the book. To all who were involved, I say thanks and the Lord's blessing on you for your crucial help.

In this book, I mention my grandchildren so allow me one small note to them. To my fantastic grandchildren, I hope this book shows you the light of Christ and the way of life that will forever guide your steps. If you trust any foundation for your life other than Jesus Christ, you will find that it is not a solid rock but sinking sand. You are blessed to have godly mothers and fathers who are continuing the faith legacy of our family. Let them teach you and guide you into abundant and everlasting life through Jesus Christ.

To my beautiful daughters and my two Godly son-in-laws, I encourage you to stay hungering and thirsting for the Lord. Don't ever give the Lord reason to accuse you of leaving your first love. Love Him with all your heart and He will give you love for one another. Remember that the greatest security you can give your children, apart from knowing Christ, is your warm love for one another.

This then is my story. When Jesus shows up, life in its most thrilling radiance is experienced. I trust this book will lift up the majesty and beauty of Jesus as it relates to our family and ministry. I want to share with my readers the miracle from heaven that transformed and continues to transform my life!

"If a man remains in me and I in him, he will bear much fruit; apart from me you can to nothing" John 15:5

Introduction

I am so glad that from the beginning of my new life in Jesus, I knew that the Christian life was something much more than a sterile religious experience. Instead, it has been a joyful, peaceful, purpose-driven and powerful Spirit-led existence which started for me in 1971. This relationship was orchestrated by the same power that raised Jesus from the dead. Can you believe it? Jesus is as much alive today as when he walked the earth. He lives in us and we are called His body. His resurrection power is what gives the strength to persevere even in difficult suffering or in painful life experiences.

I was involved in the baptism of six young Muslim men in India. These young men knew that the day they were baptized, they would be abandoned by their family and they would lose their livelihood. They were so solid in their willingness to suffer for Jesus Christ because they stood on His solid foundation.

The goal of this book is to bring glory and honor to Jesus. I know in my heart that apart from Him, apart from being in the Vine (Jesus), I can do nothing to build His Kingdom. "...No branch can bear fruit by itself; it must remain in the Vine. Neither can you bear fruit unless you remain in Me." John 15:4

This is a book about the supernatural. It is a book about the miraculous works of God. It is a book about an encounter with the living God that changed everything in our lives. My prayer for all readers would be that after you finish reading this book, you will take time to meditate on the greatness of Jesus. I hope you will fall in love with Him for the first time or renew your love for him. For you who are Christ-followers, I ask you to join in the wonderful Commission to make Christ known in the world in which we live. Enjoy the trip reading through "When Jesus Shows Up." Let it light a spark that will ignite a fire in your life. Continue the quest of fulfilling your God-designed destiny. Be a willing vessel for God to use. It's so exciting when Jesus shows up. I pray this book will honor Christ who is my life!

"No one can come to me unless the Father who sent me draws him." John 6:44

Chapter 1

The Pursuit

Being a boy raised in a farm community, I was an unlikely candidate for a transformational encounter with God. The cultural norm in our area was to attend church as a family. My mom taught Sunday School in our small church and my Dad was Santa Claus at Christmas. According to my mother, I was baptized as a baby, verified by a certificate in my baby book. At age 12, I was one of the four or five students who completed a confirmation class and became an official member of Antioch Evangelical United Brethren Church in Brookville, Ohio. The pastor read a statement of faith which I repeated phrase by phrase, and I became a member of the church. Although I may have had a faint respect for Jesus at this time, I now realize that this experience had little if any impact on my life. By the time I reached high school, my lack of commitment to this membership was demonstrated by my leaving my home church to attend a church with prettier girls. As an engineering student at General Motors Institute (GMI) in Flint, Michigan, I never darkened the door of a church in four years. My attendance dwindled to times when I was home like Easter or Christmas. Sometimes the promise of food would get me to church. At other times, it was when my mother twisted my arm or my ear to motivate me.

During this period, I did have some conversations with God. In the middle of a message one Sunday at my home church, I decided to challenge God to knock out a stained-glass window in the church as a condition to my believing in Him. He didn't so I didn't! During my time at GMI, I lived in a Greek fraternity, Phi Tau Alpha. Whatever moral character I had was quickly corrupted. Until college, I had never used alcohol. It wasn't long before I was being poured into bed or into a bath tub after a night spent partying with my fraternity brothers. I was too drunk to walk. I loved my fraternity brothers and had a close bond to them, but like me, most of them had no idea that God had a purpose for our lives. The drinking led to other bad decisions which chipped away at my own values. I did have a conscience. Unlike many of my peers, it would not let me violate the lifestyle I had been taught in my home and my church without a real struggle. For me, the consequence was shame and guilt.

I was hired by the Inland Division of General Motors at age 17, right out of high school. After completing a five year co-op program, I graduated from GMI in 1961 with an Industrial Engineering degree. Inland was a General Motors parts manufacturing company in Dayton, Ohio. This co-op program was designed for students to work eight weeks at the company and then study eight weeks at school in Flint, Michigan. My assignments after graduation would be as a Plastic Lab Engineer, a Plastics Lab Supervisor, a Design Engineer and a Staff Design Engineer. My work as a Design Engineer and then a Staff Design Engineer took me almost weekly to other GM divisions in Flint, Lansing and Detroit. I would travel by GM air shuttle or by car on these weekly trips. I would work for Inland for the next 17 years.

A story within the story is how I met my wife Judy. One of the new pledges to our fraternity was Charles Wilhelm. He had a good friend back in Dayton, Ohio that he thought I should meet. He showed me a picture of Judy and she was beautiful. I was dating another girl in Dayton at that time. Her name was Jeanie, and she was a very good friend of my sister. Jeanie and I later agreed that we had more of a brother-sister relationship than a dating relationship. I had come home from Flint for the Christmas holidays and at Charles' urging had agreed to a double date for a New Years Eve dance. Jeanie was not available for this dance due to a schedule conflict. However, her schedule changed, and she told me that she would go to dance with me. Suddenly, I had two dates for the same event. I called Charles and told him that I needed to cancel my date with Judy so I could take Jeanie to the dance. I recommended that he call another fraternity brother who needed a date to see if he would take Judy on the double date with him. Charles arranged all of this so Judy and I both ended up at the dance but with different dates. Later, I was walking across the dance floor and saw this beautiful girl whom I really wanted to meet. She evidently saw me and later I learned she had thought to herself, "Why couldn't I have come with him instead of my current date?" Neither of us knew that we were the other half of what Charles was trying to put together. When I finally saw her with Charles and my friend Dave, I knew I had to meet her. I called for a date the next evening and that started 30 straight evenings of dates. It was love at first sight for both of us. Judy was a beautiful, intelligent girl with a very high moral ethic. I fell madly in love with her on our first date. God had provided a wonderful future pastor's wife even before I needed one. We were both targets of the One who knew us and loved us even before we were born. Psalm 139:16 NIV states, "Your eyes saw my unformed body. All the days ordained for me were written in your book before one of them came to be."

After a one-and-a-half-year courtship, we married in 1962 and began to live the American dream. In the first few months after marrying, we purchased seven and a half acres in Brookville, Ohio about 15 miles north and west of Dayton. In the next three and a half years, we designed and built a new home, dug a pond, purchased two new cars and built a pen for my bird dog. What could be better? It did get much better when we brought our beautiful girls home from the hospital. Lynelle was born in 1965 and Kelly in 1968. These precious additions to our family invaded our world and we could not have been happier. We were off to grab the golden ring of prosperity and success as a young professional family.

Conviction would come to me at times to change my direction in life. I remember one such incident at the birth of my daughter Lynelle. I was banished, like all expectant fathers of that era, to the Waiting Room at the hospital. Suddenly, someone came rushing out of the Delivery Room and placed Judy's engagement and wedding rings in my hand. My gaze fastened on these rings and then on my own wedding ring. I found myself overwhelmed with shame and guilt for my own lifestyle. I began to have fearful thoughts that God would visit all my sin on this new baby girl in some kind of physical deformity. I pleaded for mercy while I spun my wedding ring on my finger. The good news is that she was born perfectly healthy. However, the growing sense of conviction of a need to change would not let me go. This common view of God as a punishing, vengeful person is frequently the view of many who are far away from Him. When we draw closer to Him, we are overwhelmed by His love and care.

My wife and my two daughters were wonderful gifts to me. How do you not believe in miracles when you first hold a newborn? I loved rocking and singing to them, playing small and big animals with them, telling Chippy (imaginary chipmunk) stories, and trapping them in my arms, giving them the idea that they had magical power to escape my traps. We fished and swam in our pond in the summer and skated on the ice in winter. I was captivated and captured by these two tiny love-filled bundles.

Over and over the thought permeated my mind that I needed to change for my girls' sake. I now understand why so many people go back to church when they have children. When I looked in the mirror, the person I saw in the reflection was not a good role model for my incredible girls. Although there was a growing sense that something needed to change in my life, I had neither the understanding nor the will power nor the discipline to do it. Year after year, I made New Year's resolutions and year after year, I broke them. I found myself asking more questions about why we were alive and if life had meaning beyond what I was experiencing. I would push these voices down to get back to my goal of climbing the corporate ladder, to do whatever it took to be successful. My education continued with an MBA from Xavier University. I was obedient to management when they suggested I not tell customers the whole truth. I did what many did on expense accounts, manipulating them to hide the huge liquor bills. I was recruited by management to do industrial espionage and actually "borrowed" a model without permission from a vendor. I drove from Dayton to Detroit to get the model, and then drove four hours back to Inland in Dayton. After a quick look at the model by our manufacturing people, I then drove it back to Detroit in the early morning hours. My efforts were lauded and I was on my way. My goal was the 14th floor of GM Central Offices in Detroit. This is the place of six-figure incomes and huge bonuses. Would this bring the ultimate fulfillment that I was seeking?

During this process of both being drawn by God and searching for truth, Judy and I, along with our two preschool girls, started back to church. I was 30 when we made this choice. We knew this would be a safe place with good moral training for the children. We purposely began a search to determine if God really existed. If He was real, what implication did this have for our lives? The church we returned to was the church of my childhood. It was more like a social club than a spiritual watering hole. The message of the gospel was not clearly stated and we became very frustrated in our search. An oft-repeated question was, if God was real, where was He in the church? We saw no evidence of His supernatural presence.

However, there was one spiritual light burning in our small church. Unknown to us, a small group of a few believers met together weekly to pray for the church. They prayed for the pastor and the people attending the church like Judy and me. Vesta Fox, Jim and Pat Siehl, and Rupert and Vi Gebhart poured out their hearts weekly that God would send renewal and revival to the church. They prayed specifically by name for us. I was notorious for spearheading the appeal to allow smoking at church fellowship events. I wanted to smoke my cigars in the church basement Fellowship Hall and we succeeded in changing the rules. What a "spiritual" achievement that was! However, the true spiritual awakening that happened at Antioch and in our lives was surely an answer to the prayers of these committed prayer warriors. God used the following encounters to draw me to Himself in this time of searching.

Encounter 1

While in Detroit on a business trip, I checked into a Holiday Inn and was preparing for an evening meeting. As was my custom when traveling, I often picked up a *Playboy Magazine*. I walked into the motel room and laid the *Playboy* down beside a *Gideon Bible* on the bedside table. The contrast caught my eye. I knew very little about the Bible, but I knew it portrayed a different lifestyle than *Playboy*. I opened the Bible by simply flipping through the pages to the book of Isaiah. I began to read and time stood still as I read all 66 chapters. It suddenly dawned on me that I was late for my meeting. I ran to the bathroom where I began to get ready. As I looked into the mirror, part of what I had just read bombarded me. In Chapter 6 Isaiah said, "Woe is me, a man of unclean lips." He was comparing himself to

God's holiness and was aware of the difference. As I looked in the mirror, I touched my lips and said to myself, "I too am a man of unclean lips." I was greatly convicted of my ungodly lifestyle and my sin. I simply didn't know what to do about it at that time.

Encounter 2

At times, an invitation was given me to eat in the Executive Dining Hall at Fisher Body Division of General Motors in Detroit. On one such day, I happened to sit next to a table where a retirement party was being given for a retiring Vice President of General Motors. I was close enough to hear what the retiree was saying. To my shock I overheard him say that if he had it to do over again, he would not have done it. He was very transparent about how his corporate life had broken apart his family. I was amazed that this man who had achieved the golden ring I was pursuing, would say that the cost of his achievements was too high. Part of my corporate dream bubble burst that day. If going up the ladder to the Vice President level isn't the path to happiness and fulfillment, what is?

Encounter 3

It was a beautiful fall day. I was early, so I was killing time before an appointment with a customer in Detroit. While doing some sightseeing, I noticed a huge junk yard with a massive car crusher in it. As I watched automobiles go into the crusher and come out as a small steel cube, it dawned on me that all my designs and hard work would end up squashed just like those cars. Was there anything to live for that would have more permanence or eternal value? The answers were soon to come.

Encounter 4

Judy's mother worked as Executive Housekeeper at a Hilton Hotel. She had bags of books at home that people had left at the motel. Judy had discovered a book by David Wilkerson, *The Cross and the Switchblade,* which she read while visiting her mother. Judy was really touched by this book and enthusiastically wanted me to read it. Later when I threw it across the room in anger, I knew she was shocked. I reacted to what I had read and felt that if God is who David Wilkerson says He was, we had no understanding of nor experience with this kind of God. David Wilkerson's God was one who spoke to him and intimately directed his life. He also powerfully transformed lives of gang leaders like Nicky Cruz. We had never heard teaching or preaching about this kind of God. Did He really exist? We were beginning to sense that we were being pursued by a God who was drawing us closer and closer to an awakening!

"You are receiving the goal of your faith, the salvation of your soul." I Peter 1:9

Chapter 2

Coming Home

One way to understand God's plan is to see it as a tapestry. When we look at the underside of the weaving, we see a tangled web of thread that has no pattern. However, when we gaze at the top, we see a beautiful pattern. My eyes were just beginning to move from the maze of meaninglessness to seeing the design that would soon become more in focus. As I learned to walk by faith, many things seemingly disassociated from one another began to have a common thread.

Salem Avenue Church of God in Dayton, Ohio was sponsoring a Lay Institute for Evangelism put on by Campus Crusade for Christ to train lay people to share their faith. A wonderful woman of God, Ruth Brayfield, was a member of this church. She was a wheelchair-bound Multiple Sclerosis (MS) patient who could still use her voice and her phone for the Lord. She was calling pastors in the Dayton area to invite them and their lay people to attend the training. Our pastor was one of those called several times.

Somewhat out of frustration because of Ruth's persistent calling, our pastor asked Judy if we could represent the church at this meeting. Judy replied that if we were available we would attend. The reason the pastor asked us was that several months before this event he had asked me to serve on the Church Council. He appointed me Evangelism Director, recognizing that this was a non-functioning position requiring nothing from me other than attending Council meetings. I had no idea what an Evangelism Director would do. I didn't know what the word evangelism meant. Since I was now holding this position, the pastor asked us to attend this conference at Salem Avenue Church of God.

My regular schedule involved weekly business trips to Detroit, so Judy knew it was fairly certain that we would not be able to attend the meeting. As the time for this conference approached, I found that all my plans to travel were cancelled. As it worked out, I could not get out of town by air, by land or by sea. On Monday, Judy reminded me of the Lay Institute beginning that evening. I told her to call the pastor and tell him we couldn't attend. She refused to do it and insisted that if I wanted to cancel, I would have to call him myself. Part of me wanted to call and decline, but part of me was curious about the event. The bottom line was that I was afraid to call the pastor since the church had paid the registration fee for each of us.

The conference was in the Church of God and that made me a little uncomfortable. I had experience with mainline denominations only. I didn't really understand the word evangelism other than to equate it with some pushy people I had known. However, strange as it may seem, on Monday evening we were reluctantly in our seats at the Lay Institute of Evangelism. Over 2500 people came to the training, and that posed a problem because the church could not seat that many people. It was a mass of humanity. The planners obviously did not know of Ruth Brayfield's persistence. A crisis call went out to Campus Crusade Staff all over the Midwest and many started making their way to Dayton, Ohio. As staff became available, the conference was split into two groups, one in the morning and one in the evening.

Everyone could feel the electricity in the air as the meeting on Monday evening was opened with prayer. I heard some of the first gospel songs other than traditional hymns that I had ever heard. One in particular touched me. It was *His Name is Wonderful*. I still get chills up and down my spine when I hear it today. The evening speaker was Howard Ball, the National Lay Director of Campus Crusade. I learned that his background was in "underground condominiums" which is code for a salesman of funeral plots. As he began to speak, I was enthralled. No sooner had he started to share when a man stood up and started speaking in tongues. I had never heard this before. Even though it was scary, it also whetted my appetite for the supernatural. Howard rebuked the man for being out of order, but for me this was not a turn-off. This was the first supernatural sign that I had ever experienced in a church meeting.

Looking back, after Howard had shared his personal testimony, I realized that he had touched on everything I was looking for in my life. He had found forgiveness, purpose, peace and power for his life in the person of Jesus Christ. He then quoted Revelation 3:20 where Jesus said, "Here I am! I stand at the door and knock. If anyone hears my voice and opens the door, I will come in and eat with him and he with me." I began to hear the knocking on the door of my life. It would grow louder and more persistent in the following three days.

After that session, we were divided into smaller groups to practice sharing our faith. Tom Spencer was my facilitator from Campus Crusade for Christ. He distributed a booklet called *The Four Spiritual Laws* and began going through it. This immediately touched me. He started by reading, "God loves you and has a wonderful plan for your life." How could God love me when I didn't like myself? Then Tom talked about our sin problem, of Jesus dying for our sins, and of our need to ask Him into our lives through faith. Little by little, the tapestry was starting to show a design.

As we drove home Monday night, Judy and I were uncomfortably quiet. We were only speaking of trivia and both of us were mulling over what we had heard, but we were not ready to talk about what was happening to us. I started to have my first "counting the cost" thoughts. If I gave my life to Christ, how would it affect my job? How would it cramp my entertainment of customers and how would it effect the way I filled out expense accounts? What would our family and friends think of us? Thus, a two-day wrestling match with God began, a match I was destined to lose.

Returning for the Tuesday evening session, we mingled with fellow conference attendees prior to the starting time. I was asked by a stranger, "How long have you been a Christian?" Twenty-four hours earlier, I would have said, "All of my life." I would have told them I was baptized and confirmed. Now I was strangely silent before this man's question. I walked away to avoid the answer. For the first time I had a growing understanding that even though I was attending a church and on the Church Council, I was not a Christian. We experienced another evening learning to share *The*

Four Spiritual Law booklet followed by another silent drive home. Another night and day of wrestling with the radical call of Christ on my life was unsettling yet brought hope in a way I didn't understand.

The struggle continued through Wednesday. On Wednesday evening, we were introduced to the concept of the indwelling Holy Spirit. We learned we could experience the same power that raised Jesus from the dead. In a film clip, Bill Bright, President of Campus Crusade said, "It is impossible to live the Christian Life." I was trying to decide whether to give my life to Christ and now I am told the life is impossible. Then Bill threw out the hook and said, "Unless Jesus Christ lives His resurrected life in and through you, you can't live it." Once again, I was faced with the supernatural. I sensed that men like Dr. Bill Bright and Rev. David Wilkerson knew something I didn't, but I was deeply attracted to their kind of God and was developing a great thirst to experience Him.

Judy and I had our usual quiet drive home. Judy wanted to check some Scripture quotes from Howard Ball out of Romans 7. To Judy, the reading had portrayed her own struggles as if the author knew her, but could she really trust what the speaker was saying? When she confirmed the teaching in her own reading of the Bible, her heart was opening up to what she had been hearing.

My wrestling took me out to our pond late in the evening. It was a beautiful starlit night. All creation seemed brilliant and alive. I looked up and began a conversation that would forever change me. I told God that I had been running my own life for 33 years and I wasn't proud of the results. I acknowledged my sin and asked for His forgiveness. I invited Him into my life with a prayer, but with very little faith. I said, "Jesus if you are real, come into my life and make me what you want me to be." That tiny mustard seed of faith was enough!

Five people had been praying, Ruth Brayfield refused to give up, Howard Ball had shared a powerful testimony, Tom Spencer had opened the Scriptures to me and the Holy Spirit had pounded on my heart. Best yet, I asked Jesus to come into my life and He came!!! In a moment, I was a new creation. I went into the house and dusted off an old King James Version of the Bible. Even with the antiquated English, the Bible came to life. Unknown to me, Judy asked Christ into her life within 24 hours after my prayer. Now we were no longer quiet. We were told there were 7,000 promises in the New Testament for a new believer. In the first few weeks after the conference, we tried to find all 7,000.

Many wanted to know what my conversion experience felt like. I had no great emotional experience. What had happened was founded more on God's promises than on my feelings, promises like John 10:10, "I have come that they may have life, and have it to the full." This was foundational to what happened to us. In our emptiness, His fullness came. If there was a feeling at all, it was that I had been on a long journey and I finally returned home where I belonged! I was at peace and at home in the arms of my Lord and Savior, Jesus Christ. On October 15, 1971, God answered the prayers of five praying saints and Jesus showed up. Judy and I are eternally grateful to them and to Him.

"Therefore, if anyone is in Christ, he is a new creation; the old has gone, the new has come." II Corinthians 5:17

Chapter 3

New Life Changes Everything

The first day of a new life is exhilarating! On my first day as a new Christian, God's grace was very evident. It was a very strange day starting with a new awareness of the beauty of creation. Previously, I had loved to argue with Christians about evolution and creation. Today the argument was over! I now believed in a Creator who spoke life into being and was awed by the grandeur of all that I saw. Being mesmerized all the way to work with the sense of God's presence, I felt truly alive in a way I had never experienced before.

As I entered my office at Inland Division of General Motors in Dayton, Ohio where I was supervising seven engineers, I viewed these people in a new way. They were no longer pawns to walk over on the way to the top, but real people with real needs, hurts and dreams. Suddenly, I wanted to know who they were and how I could help them achieve their goals. I had always respected them because of what they brought to our team, but my interest in them was always in the context of the job. Now they were more than fellow workers. I wanted to get to know their wives and children. I wondered if some of my fellow Inland employees longed for a more fulfilling life. Were they ready for new life in Christ?

In trying to invoke some spirited conversation, I remember putting a Campus Crusade book entitled *The Uniqueness of Jesus* on my desk. I hoped someone would ask me about it. Eventually it did spawn conversations with employees. A few days before, it would have been appalling to me to do something like that. Chapter 4 will tell more about the Inland story and how God used the following two years to influence people at Inland and beyond.

As my work day ended, I drove home. Upon reaching my driveway at home, I parked the car and walked to our house. During this short walk, I felt as if someone tapped me on the shoulder and I heard a very quiet inner voice say, "Your wife gives and gives and gives and you take and take and take." My immediate reaction was not to like this kind of meddling in my life! The more I thought about this message, the more I realized that a loving God had just given me an impression of some of the transformation He desired to do in my life. His desire was to lead us into the marriage He had designed for us, not the one we had been living. We have been on that journey for over 55 years together. His design was that Judy and I would love one another the way Christ loves His church. I learned that I had to experience God's love before I could ever love the way He does.

This was the first day of the rest of my life. I had escaped darkness to come into a wonderful light. Our lives began to be a whirl of Christian activity. We were at church, a Bible study or at Campus Crusade events frequently. We had such a burden to learn, to grow and to understand more about God's plan for our lives. As we grew in Christ, we grew closer together.

Campus Crusade

As new believers, we had so many questions that were not or could not be answered in our home church. Our frustration level grew. Over several months, Judy cried out to God and told him that if she didn't get some answers quickly, she wouldn't continue to follow Christ. Right on God's schedule, she received a call from John Lynch, a Campus Crusade staff member from Michigan. Judy had met him at the Lay Institute in Dayton. He asked her if we could provide some lodging for him on his next trip into our area. He knew of our decision to follow Christ. A major motivation for his trip was to work with pastors who had people trained in the Lay Institute of Evangelism so they could make a great impact on the city of Dayton and beyond. He also wanted to help new believers like us in the Dayton area to become firmly grounded in God's Word.

He was like a breath of fresh air when he arrived. He came with candy in his hands for our daughters and with rich spiritual food in his heart and mind for us. Finally, someone could answer many of our questions even the silly ones such as, "If John the Baptist was the Elijah who was to come, does the Bible teach reincarnation?" John stayed with us for several days and would teach us late into the night. John and his wife, Sharon, have remained great friends and mentors over many years. Although we have always lived far apart geographically, they pop back into our lives when we truly need them.

One night as we finished our question and answer session, John and I went out to our pond to cool off with a swim. We were floating on some large inner tubes on the water looking toward the dark night sky. The stars seemed so much brighter than normal and majestic beyond description with their heavenly light. John began to rejoice that we knew the Creator of this entire Universe and that He loved us so much that He came to earth in the person of his Son and died on the cross for us. We sang and rejoiced, and it was one of the most memorable worship experiences of my life. I was learning already the power of praise and to experience the joy of the Lord.

John began to challenge us to be part of the Campus Crusade Lay Ministry. He recruited us to come to Lay Institutes for Evangelism as helpers. My first assignment was to move books in and out of conference sites for the book table. John would always tell me as I carried books, "You are laying up gold in Heaven!" Judy worked at the registration table. It wasn't long until John had us sharing our testimony in the seminars and then he closely followed this with releasing us to lead the Lay Evangelism Training, the Evangelistic Bible Study Training and the class on Using Your Home for Evangelistic Entertaining. We loved our association with these people who were so passionate for Jesus and were like elite commandos in the Lord's army.

Campus Crusade was the largest missionary organization in the world in the 1970's. Hundreds of thousands came to Christ during these years. Thousands of lay people in hundreds of churches were trained to share their faith. The "JESUS" film was made and has resulted in more conversions around the world than any other single evangelistic tool. Judy and I had finally found something to live for that was worth dying for if necessary. Our goal in life was now to get the gospel out to unreached people so all men and women everywhere will worship and glorify God.

One evening while going to the grocery with John, we were standing in the check-out line. In front of us was a young African-American man who had on a Black Power tee shirt with a clenched fist on the back. He looked tough and foreboding. John opened a conversation with him and in a short time this man was crying and asking Jesus Christ into his life. This was a powerful modeling of a committed Christian lifestyle for us.

These experiences had us continuously sharing our faith with those around us. Once Judy was invited to speak to a group of Lutheran pastors' wives. After she had shared her testimony, she presented the *Four Spiritual Laws* to them. Two thirds of this group prayed to receive Christ and for some it was the first time they had any assurance of their salvation.

My job had me flying frequently. It was not unusual for me to have the opportunity to talk to people about the Lord on these flights. On one particular flight, I was seated next to a young Muslim man. We got into a deep conversation about the things of God. I asked him to share with me his Muslim faith and then I would share with him my Christian faith. I remember that just as our plane touched the runway at our destination, this man was asking Christ into his life. I sensed that God had really touched him deeply.

As a result of intensive discipleship training, we began to experience a most exciting and fulfilling life. Judy enrolled in the Salem Avenue Evangelism Training program and I began a Bible Study in the Engineering Department at Inland. We also started a Bible Study with our neighbors. We began attending Salem Ave. Church of God because they were the church that housed the Lay Institute of Evangelism. Dr. David Grubbs, the pastor, (see Chapter 6) became a wonderful mentor and friend.

The Inland Bible Study

As a brand new believer, I did not know a lot about the Word of God, the Bible. However, I knew it was changing my life so I wanted to share it with those with whom I worked. I remember going to meet with two draftsmen at Inland named David Ludwig and Jim Wilhide. I had a suspicion they might be Christians by observing their lifestyle. I found out they were followers of Christ. I asked them if they would lead a noon Bible study in the Engineering Department. Neither one was willing to take this leadership role, but both said they would be supportive for me to lead it and that they would attend. I picked up some Campus Crusade materials called the *10 Basic Steps of Christian Living* and we began a fill-in-the-blank Bible study.

The group started with four men and grew to about 30. We met once a week on our lunch hour. God began to strengthen these men. They became bolder and more excited about their faith. Because of this study, God was able to introduce His Son to several engineers. This group was started in early 1972 and even though I left Inland in 1973, the Bible Study was still meeting in 2008. It is amazing how seeds planted for the Kingdom grow and multiply greatly becoming fruitful beyond expectations.

The Neighborhood Study

As we grew in our faith, we also wanted to share it with our neighbors. We invited Emerson and Wanda Steck and Jim and Betty Locker to an evangelistic Bible study in our home. These neighbors were already good friends, but this took our friendship to a different level. We watched in awe as God touched their lives and set their hearts on fire like he had ours. Every Memorial Day, Fourth of July and Labor Day, all of us got together with a few other neighbors for a picnic. We began ending our time together singing hymns and telling of the Lord's greatness. The David Dutter family who were from an Old Order German Baptist Church joined us also. David and Jane Dutter and their four children became great friends and pilgrims with us on our spiritual journey. David and Jane have made it to Heaven before us, as has Emerson Steck. We look forward to a great reunion! The Steck family and Locker family and the Dutter's children are all wonderful friends to this day. When we go back to Brookville we always see many of them. These families and their adult children are following Christ and are having a great impact for the Kingdom.

Our Family

The place we made our biggest mistake was with our immediate family. We were very passionate for the Lord, but we were not very mature or wise. I immediately shared the *Four Spiritual Laws* with my mom and dad. I was so zealous in sharing what had happened to me that my mother and father left feeling in some way that we no longer accepted them as they were. Secondly, my mother felt chagrined that we would even suggest that someone like herself who had taught Sunday School for many years might not have been a Christian.

After this bad start, we got some wonderful advice. A friend advised us to show our parents the love of Christ by serving them rather than preaching to them. It wasn't very long until my mom pinned a *Four Spiritual Laws* booklet on my pillow that showed that she knew for certain that Christ was in her life and that she had eternal life. Dad made his way to Christ also and both died with Jesus on their lips.

For Judy's mom, it would take many years, but she did accept Christ in her 80's. Judy was able to lead her Dad to Christ shortly before his death in his 70's. This was a great miracle as he had a hardened agnostic heart at best and a great hatred for the church. He was raised Catholic where he was an altar boy and he despised his roots. After he prayed to receive Christ, his nurses saw a great change in his behavior in the nursing home. Leo wanted Judy's mom to read scripture to him when she came to visit. What a change!

My sister Joyce was a wonderful person who had attended church her entire life and like our mother she taught Sunday school for many years. Her heart was so open for the things of God that when Judy and I begin to follow Christ, Joyce began to really grow and understand the gospel of Christ in a life-transforming way. She lived the rest of her life as an incredible witness to the grace of God and many were touched by her life. She has already had a reunion with our parents in Heaven and I know she rejoices with those who have gone before her in our family. At her funeral, Joyce's neighbor and friend said, "I thought I was a Christian until I met a real one," speaking of Joyce. You could not miss the fact that Jesus had shown up in her life and that she was a light to the world.

"Blessed are those who are persecuted because of righteousness for theirs is the kingdom of heaven."
Matthew 5:10

Chapter 4

The Clash of Two Worlds

Deciding to follow Christ comes with the strong possibility of great personal cost. Little did I know the challenges that would come because of my new walk with God. As soon as I became a Christian, I felt that God had captured my heart, but in my mind I was still wrestling with doubt. I was fighting the memory bank in my mind which held all my unbelief and my pagan roots. As I flew almost every week to Detroit, Michigan and back again to Dayton, I would regularly read a small *Living Bible* New Testament. This book would convict me of many of my habits and attitudes. I would at times question, "Am I on some new kind of psychological trip?" Then God would again warm my heart to draw me to Him, especially as I began to confess my doubt as sin and receive His forgiveness.

I identified with Luke 9:4, "I do believe; help me overcome my unbelief!" The voices of my parents and in-laws would haunt me. They felt we had gone off the deep end. Even though my mother had taught Sunday School all of her life and had even prayed at one time that her son would be a minister, she was initially uncomfortable with the radical change in my life.

Judy's father had gone around his neighborhood telling people his son-in-law had gone crazy. But as I shared earlier, both sets of parents would come to know the Christ we loved, and my mother would eventually become one of the greatest supporters in our ministry.

It was at this time that I read two books that would bring my heart and mind into one accord: *Mere Christianity* by C. S. Lewis and *The Normal Christian Life* by Watchman Nee. These two books were instrumental in answering many of the difficult questions that were causing doubt. They helped me see both God's grand design for my life and to see my identity in Christ.

Conflict at Inland Division of General Motors

After a few months of being a Christian, I was in our usual Friday meeting at Inland which we actually called our "Pack of Lies" meeting. One of our largest product lines was in jeopardy because competitors had developed a very good product to challenge us. We were in a stalling mode with our customer, Fisher Body, trying to rapidly develop a new product to overcome this threat. Since progress was slow, we were trying to find any possible way to buy time. Our dishonesty was more in what we did not share with Fisher Body than in what we did share. I was the spokesman for our company with this customer. It was our largest dollar-volume product. As I sat in the back of the meeting preparing for the next week of diversionary tactics, a strange thought entered my mind. There was a strong impression that I could no longer be part of the deception that had been our standard operational procedure. The message was becoming very clear. I knew the days of misleading our customer were over. However, I was afraid to say anything about this impression in the larger meeting of our top management personnel.

Later I went in to my Supervisor and told him of my decision. I could no longer be part of the deception that had been our practice. I fully realized that walking in the door with this information could have put my job in jeopardy. I remembered that my boss had once told me he had given serious consideration to the Catholic priesthood. Therefore, I was hopeful that with this history he would understand my dilemma. He listened to my story with very little body or facial response except for puffing on his pipe. It seemed like an eternity before he spoke. Finally, he said, "I need to think about this awhile. In the meantime, I will make the call on the customer next week until we can talk this through." Even though I was praying continuously about this situation, I had to fight off waves of fear and insecurity.

We didn't speak again until the middle of the next week. Time stood still; five days seemed like five weeks. I certainly talked to God a lot that week. Finally, after several days, I learned that my boss had initiated a conversation with his superiors. They all recognized that I had a closer relationship with our customer than anyone else in the company. I had developed great friendships and relationships with several levels of Engineering Management plus those in Purchasing at Fisher Body. Inland could not afford to lose those relationships at this critical time. Engineering Management agreed to give me a green light to share where we actually were on our product development. Looking back, I think I was given a coil of rope and some, no doubt, hoped I would hang myself. Some knew we needed a change because what we had been doing was no longer successful. Amazingly, my boss finally told me that we would be transparent and honest with the customer. He also told me that if my truth telling backfired or blew up, both he and I would probably be fired as Inland employees.

The first meeting with our customer after this decision was very frightening to me. I was very uneasy about the outcome and what the consequences could be. As I was praying, I found a sense of peace and expectancy. Obviously, I couldn't tell them that we had been misleading them. I simply told them the truth about where we were in the process. After the meeting, a Chief Engineer called me into his office. He insisted that he know what was different about me. He kept pushing me and pushing me. With fear and trepidation, I gave him my testimony. To my amazement, he affirmed that he was also a believer, and rejoiced in my decision. He told me that the fact we were both Christians didn't mean that we would get the business we sought, but he also said that from that day on he would believe what I told him. Things could have gone very differently that day. However, the outcome was that we worked very hard, developed a better product, and actually increased the percentage of our business with this customer. To God be the glory!

Not long after that meeting at Fisher Body, a conviction came to me regarding the way expense accounts were being handled at Inland. Although we were expected to wine and dine the customers, liquor bills were not permitted on expense sheets. This conflict of conscience versus company policy forced me to take a trip to the Accounting Office. Existing guidelines promoted padding of expense accounts so that liquor bills were covered by other line items. The policy was actually causing employees to be dishonest and very probably causing the company to spend more. I appealed to those responsible for setting the policy for expense accounts. Sitting down with an Accounting Supervisor, I told him why I felt his guidelines were not producing the results he had desired. I told him I could no longer support this policy and that I was going to tell all my Plastics Lab Engineers to turn in exactly what they spent and not try to make it fit some arbitrary guideline. I suggested to Accounting that I felt they would actually come out ahead if they would make a change in this policy. People would no longer have to lie and cheat. The new policy change was ultimately made, and new expense account procedures were adopted. At least eight of us stopped padding expense accounts which had been the common procedure for years. Never would I have done this before Jesus became my moral compass. It was His wonderful grace that brought the change.

Another challenge came from one of my best friends. He was my boss's immediate supervisor and was an Assistant Chief Engineer. He and I had been really good drinking buddies for years, and he had been instrumental in me getting my latest promotion. He told me when I was promoted that it was due to my reputation in our industrial espionage ventures. He said I was a good enough liar to do a great job. When my life began to change, my friend was furious. He would come to my desk and would purposely use the Lord's name in vain. He started calling me every Monday, right before the Bible study I was leading for Engineers, asking me to do some mundane task even though I was on my own time. It became obvious that he was just trying to force me to leave the Bible study. To confront him could have ended my employment. After our entire Bible study prayed for my appeal, I went to him, told him what the Bible study meant to me and to the other men. I invited him to attend which he quickly turned down. Again, God intervened because my friend stopped harassing me.

A personal issue began to surface. I was a workaholic. I usually came in earlier and stayed later than anyone else. Now I wanted a life of balance with job, family and personal time. Realizing that Inland was no longer the source of my income brought a great breakthrough for me. My source was now God himself who had promised to meet my needs and the needs of my family. I think I became a much more balanced and productive employee when I began to seek God's priorities rather than my own.

A problem that was a growing concern for me was my entertaining of customers into the wee hours of the morning in Detroit. When Christ came into my life, I knew that I could no longer drink until I was drunk. I started limiting my drinking to one or two drinks an evening. This continued for about six months. One day, when I was sitting in a restaurant with a drink in my hand, a man walked into the bar who looked just like a man I had led to the Lord that past week in Dayton, Ohio. I felt convicted that this would not have been a good witness to him and that was the end of my drinking. I still entertained customers and bought them drinks, but the bills were noticeably less than they were before I entered into the life of Christ.

I know there was talk at Inland about "Preacher John." I was not yet involved in professional ministry, but often two or three of us would make the four-hour drive to Detroit and drive back the next day. Some of my partners in travel were Christians, but most were not. It almost got to be a joke about my pulpit on wheels. I did have the opportunity to speak into many lives and I found out later that some of those talks had eternal benefit. Some of the people who traveled with me soon joined our Bible study and began to grow as Christians. I also valued my opportunities to share with my colleagues at Fisher Body where I went about 90% of the time I traveled. God just kept leading me to people who were hurting or sick and needed prayer and encouragement.

After a period of time, my weekly business travel to Detroit and all my involvements in various Christian endeavors at home brought feelings of tension between ministry and my job. Judy and I were very involved as teachers in Campus Crusade's Ministry. We were also in the evangelism program of a local church plus morning and evening Sunday worship. I remember telling God what He already knew, that I needed to back off either on ministry or my job. One of these had to go because I was feeling the pressure of trying to do both. The Lord would use the conflict of job responsibilities and personal ministry to initiate the destruction of a good engineering career. I was set free to follow a call to full-time ministry which I share in Chapter 5.

Leaving Inland

It was two years after my conversion that I left my Staff Engineering position at Inland. My departure lead to two going away parties, one in Dayton at Inland and one in Detroit at Fisher Body. The hand of God was very obvious on both of these events. I had planned to leave my Inland position in September of 1973 and give a one-month notice late in the summer. However, I became aware that I was to be promoted to a new position and that my promotion was going to involve moving three or four people. I couldn't, in good conscience, remain silent about my plans to leave in three months. I decided to inform Inland's management about my plans to enter Seminary. I needed to continue my income until September to make our finances work. By telling Inland Management in June, I knew they could have asked me to leave immediately. Instead they graciously allowed me to continue working until September. Once more, I sensed the provision of the Lord.

For 17 years I had been employed at Inland Division of GM, so the theme of my retirement party was "17 and Out." Some friends who were planning the party came to me and told me that they had a problem. They knew I didn't drink, but if they didn't have beer at the retirement party, some people wouldn't come. I told them I wanted as many people there as they could possibly get because I would have a chance to explain why I was leaving and what had happened in my life. I couldn't believe the great turnout. It was an awesome evening. No one got drunk, everyone heard my testimony and I had a chance to tell them how they could receive Christ. Some came up to me afterword to tell me of their changed lives because I had shared Christ with them previously.

The party at Fisher Body was a boat trip on the Detroit River followed by dinner at a riverfront restaurant with a huge piano bar. We sat in a group of about 25 people around this piano bar. I had prayed very hard that I would have a chance for a final testimony to these men, some of whom I had shared with previously. I had some great one-on-one conversations and then it was dinner time. The Lord put a man beside me who had taken a few too many drinks and was fairly loud. He began to ask me questions that allowed me to share the gospel with all around the table. Everyone listened, and the entire bar got quiet as he asked questions like, "Why didn't God choose me instead of you?" and "Why would God love me?" He wanted to know, "What is so special about Jesus?" He followed with, "Is there any hope for a sinner like me?" As is obvious, his questions opened the door for God to answer my prayers. It was amazing to me that "God choose the foolish things of the world to shame the wise; God chose the weak things of the world to shame the strong." (I Corinthians 1:27 NIV) The drunkest man at the table was the instrument of God to answer my prayer. What a mighty God we serve! When Jesus joins us, nothing is impossible!

> *"The Lord came and stood there calling as at other times
> "Samuel! Samuel!" Then Samuel said,
> "Speak, for your servant is listening." I Samuel 3:10*

Chapter 5

The Call

There is a wonderful biblical truth that came out of Martin Luther's Reformation which emphasized the priesthood of all believers. This was an affirmation that all of us have the opportunity to minister as Christians. Some will do this as tent-makers, holding down a full-time job, while others will be set apart to put all their energies and efforts into building the Kingdom of God. Although we are all called to Christian ministry, this call to be set apart as a missionary, church planter or pastor is usually very specifically given by God and is recognized by the body of believers.

It was about one year into our new Christian life when Judy and I both began to sense that my days as an engineer were coming to an end. I remember investigating the Intercristo website (https://intercristo.wordpress.com/) to see what full-time ministry opportunities were available around the world. The early part of this awareness was really a desire to put more time and energy into the Lord's work. There was a growing feeling of being limited in my ministry due by my travel schedule and the great pressure of my job. After going to the altar at our church one Sunday morning to pray about this, Rev. Roger Brewer, Associate Pastor at Salem Avenue Church of God, came to pray with me. He tried to talk me out of leaving my job by telling me how much we needed committed Christians in the business world. This was a concern I had prayed much about, but still felt the urging of the Holy Spirit to leave my job. I got the same advice from family members and others with whom I shared my struggle.

Judy was very open to this whole process as long as I didn't move toward pastoral ministry. She had grown up in an overly critical church where pastors were chewed up and spit out on a regular basis. She saw her pastors and their wives filled with pain, hurt and frustration. Because of this background, she wanted nothing to do with life in the fish bowl called pastoral ministry. She would have quickly said yes to joining Campus Crusade for Christ, but being a pastor's wife conjured up difficult past memories.

I was asked by friends in Campus Crusade to visit a pastor in Dayton, Ohio to follow up on the Lay Institute. This pastor had wanted to start an evangelism program in his church and I was sent there to discuss this with him. The appointment was set for 8:00 PM and I was still with him at midnight. He had poured out his broken heart over his own sense of failure. On the drive home early in the morning, I was heavily burdened for this pastor. The ten mile drive to my home would change the rest of my life. God spoke to my heart and impressed upon me that he wanted shepherds who were not defeated and discouraged to lead and encourage His people. It was through this pastor's hurt and pain that God birthed a ministry in me. I could hardly keep my car on the road. It was so exciting to know that God wanted me to be a pastor. This joy in knowing God's direction for me was in sharp contrast to the dismay and anger of Judy when I told her what I felt God was saying. There was little question that unless God put her mind at ease about this direction, it would be foolish to proceed. Thus began a 18 month battle for Judy. She finally came kicking and screaming to surrender to God's plan. We now feel God's timing was set by Judy's struggle. We knew we could not do this without coming together in a unified call. She became a wonderful pastor's wife!

A group of people from Salem Avenue Church were scheduled to take a trip to Israel. I asked them to pray for us while they were in the Garden of Gethsemane. We needed clarification about God's call, plan and timing for our lives. The Sunday after they returned from Israel, Dr. David Grubbs preached a sermon called *Oh Jerusalem, Oh Jerusalem*. I was propelled to the altar at the end of the message. That morning I finally made the decision to leave my job in the fall and start a new journey. It was very frightening and yet extremely exhilarating. It is interesting that I again met Roger Brewer at the altar and this time he encouraged me to follow the call that I was sensing. Judy had surrendered to this call, but she was honest about her feelings as I went down the aisle that morning. She wanted to tackle me to stop the process. She knew this would bring great challenges and changes to her life. We immediately began the process to plan for our pursuit of pastoral ministry to start in the fall of 1973.

Seminary training was a necessity since I had no Bible school training or any kind of pastoral ministry training. A highly technical engineering degree and an

MBA degree did not prepare me adequately for ministry. My desire was to attend Asbury Seminary and study under Dr. Robert Coleman. His book, *Master Plan of Evangelism,* was one of the best books ever written on discipleship. However, when Judy and I traveled to Wilmore, Kentucky, it became obvious that there were no jobs available for Judy, a kindergarten teacher. Kindergarten was to become available the following school year. This was not the outcome for which we had hoped.

In the meantime, Dr. Grubbs had been working with Anderson School of Theology (SOT) in Anderson, Indiana, to see if they would allow me to commute the 85 miles between Dayton and Anderson to attend seminary. They agreed for Randy Rohr who was Youth Pastor at our church and me to commute together twice a week. We were responsible for the third class each week which was recorded for our study. We logged 340 miles per week to attend seminary during the next three years. I also took additional courses at United Theological Seminary in Dayton, Ohio. That way I was able to get a Master of Divinity degree in a little less than three years.

Judy and I continued to live in our much loved home in Brookville, Ohio. Dr. Grubbs had offered me the position of Evangelism/Discipleship Director at Salem Avenue Church of God. My heart was passionate about seeing people come to Christ and it was a wonderful church for my own training and development. Making all of $100 per week, I was to work 20 hours per week. Dr. Grubbs had built a strong evangelistic ministry at the church and he brought me in to lead this ministry. He and I worked together, and the Evangelism

Explosion Ministry grew to about 150 people involved. Our teams went out weekly to share the good news of the gospel with church visitors and people in the community. This was the heartbeat of this exciting growing church.

We also started small group discipleship cells for the nurture of believers and for outreach to others. We spent one year training seven couples to lead small groups at Salem. Judy and I led this training group with many who became our best friends. They went on to lead small groups that made a great impact on the church.

Our final responsibility was to teach a New Christian Class in our Sunday morning Sunday School hour. These new believers were so excited to be growing in the Lord. We have done this throughout our ministry because new believers are very hungry for the Lord and need to be encouraged and built up. Some of the most powerful Bible studies we have experienced are with new Christians.

From Yuppie to Pauper

Engineering jobs tend to offer good money. On top of that, I was now in the bonus group at GM, the point at which compensation really escalates. We had more than what we needed financially. Knowing that we were eventually leaving Inland, I calculated how much money would be needed to make it through three years of seminary. We had some retirement savings that could be tapped if needed and we had other resources that could be used to make it through the coming three years

Judy had formerly been a kindergarten teacher and was told by her previous school district that they would love to have her back. However, after waiting from April to August with no resignations, there was no job to offer. We needed her income to be able to make this transition. She quickly checked with neighboring school districts only to find all positions had been filled.

Several other actions were taken at this time. We knew we couldn't afford to continue to live in our country home, so we put our house on the market and had a duplex built for us in Dayton. Our intention was to live in one side of the duplex and rent the other out, hopeful that it could be a good long-term investment. I felt like this could always be insurance for us to have no matter where God eventually called us. We put our country home on the market and I took some of my savings and made a down payment on a brand new duplex. Unfortunately, our house went on the market at a time when interest rates on home loans rapidly rose to 18%. No houses were selling because huge down payments were required. In the meantime, our duplex was completed, and we put the "for rent" sign in the front yard. The picture at this time was not good. Judy had no job; our income was $100 per week and the duplex was draining our resources rapidly.

Some other stress came because we had purchased two new cars on GM's Executive Purchase Plan. The total amount for these two cars purchased the previous January was due shortly after Christmas. We had always bought one or two new cars per year and would get such a good up-front discount that we could sell them a year later with little or nothing owed. We knew this large payment was coming, but with everything else not going as planned, the situation got very serious. We needed reliable cars for our commuting, so we paid for them. This drained us of a huge amount of capital reserves. The duplex didn't rent even with advertising, so the cars and the duplex were the straws that broke the camel's back.

As we began to run out of money, we grew a large garden so we could survive on items we canned or put in our freezer. My parents frequently fed us which helped us greatly. Things continued to spiral downward until we had little food in the house. I remember expressing to God, "If you treat your friends like this, it's no wonder that you do not have more friends." He was very silent and chose not to respond to this charge. Judy had become increasingly depressed over our lack of funds and her inability to get a job. She was able to substitute as a teacher about twice a week, but this paid very little. We came to the point where we nearly ran out of hope. I persuaded my downcast wife to get out from under her blue blanket long enough to have a family prayer meeting. We invited our two little girls, now in kindergarten and second grade to pray. The girls didn't last long before going to bed and Judy followed shortly thereafter. We had been crying out about our needs to God and asking Him to intervene.

Now I was alone, feeling strongly my need to provide for my family. As I sat before the Lord, I broke. I asked God to show me if I had been missing Him in some way or if there was sin in my life that had been hindering us. Over the next few minutes, I enjoyed the most gentle ministry of the Holy Spirit that I had ever known. God lovingly began to show me that first, my heart wasn't right because I certainly wasn't rejoicing in all things. Next He dealt with my tendency to try to do good things for God without finding out if they really were His will. In my mind I heard, "Did I direct you to buy the duplex?" Did I tell you to sell your house? Why are you complaining about my provision when you haven't listened to me?" I didn't hear these words audibly but I heard them deep within my heart and mind. I immediately repented and agreed with God. I remember telling him that as long as my family had a roof over our head and food, I would not complain. As I gave the house, the duplex, and the job situation to Him, I experienced an incredible peace. Somehow, I knew a great work had been done even though nothing had changed in our circumstances.

About this same time, Judy was given some powerful revelation in her daily devotional about the Israelites grieving God as they traveled in the wilderness. It was their grumbling and mumbling that angered God. She shared this with me, and we both knew immediately we had become like the Israelites. We both felt the urgency to repent of these attitudes and to live in a spirit of thanksgiving and expectancy.

Feeding by the Ravens

In ancient Israel, a prophet by the name of Elijah was used by God to bring great witness to the power and majesty of God. As he was in preparation for an encounter with the false god Baal, the Bible says that Elijah was fed twice per day by the ravens. (I Kings 17:6) Like Elijah, we had a season of God's provision that was beyond anything we had ever known. We felt very thankful as we continued to live in our country home. Looking back, we know now that our house was not meant to sell. It continued to be our home for four more years. Our house on the hill proved to be a place God would use greatly, delivering many teenagers and young adults from drugs. Jesus illustrated the power of our witness when he said, "You are the light of the world. A city on a hill cannot be hidden. Neither do people light a lamp and put it under a bowl. Instead they put it on its stand, and it gives light to everyone in the house. In the same way, let your light shine before men, that they may see your good deeds and praise your Father in heaven." (Matthew 5:14-16)

Not long after that, Judy was informed about the need for a kindergarten teacher at the beginning of the second semester. She was quickly hired, and the job was exactly what she wanted. She would remain in this job until we went to Dallas in 1977. Both sides of our duplex rented, and we later decided to sell it. Both units stayed rented until the day it was sold. As these financial pressures were eased along with our grumbling attitude, people we didn't know, people we had taught, or people who had heard our testimony began to send us checks in the mail. There would always be a "God told us to" note. We were amazed at God's provision. Two brothers at Inland, Charlie and Glen Arthur, who also attended Salem, started giving us their Cost-of-Living checks every quarter. This was very hard for me to accept since they were blue collar workers who didn't have large salaries. This proved to be part of God's process of dealing with our pride.

Our families, who really weren't initially supportive of our ministry, were used by God in various ways to help resource those early ministry years. We are deeply grateful for all of these family members, friends, and

Christian brothers and sisters who were so supportive. God still sends the ravens to feed us!

The Park Place Experience

As you can surmise from the previous discussion, God was shaping and training us to live a life of faith. Another "Aha" experience happened in seminary. I was sitting quietly and meditating in the sanctuary of Park Place Church of God in Anderson. Gazing around at this large campus church, an overwhelming feeling of inadequacy engulfed me. Looking at all the seats and realizing that Greek and Hebrew scholars and people with PhDs in Theology would be sitting in these seats on Sunday morning became very intimidating. Satan was using this situation to try one more time to stop my ministry. The words flying through my mind were, "Who are you to preach in a place like this? Who deceived you to believe that you could lead this or any other church?" I began to think how ridiculous this whole call-of-God thing was and wondered if I could get my job back in engineering. There would only be one more time in my entire journey that I would have this thought. I closed my eyes to try to drown out the growing turmoil in my soul. I called out the name of Jesus multiple times and soon I felt a growing sense of peace. The disconcerting voice was stilled.

A vivid impression came with Jesus saying, "I never called you to lead a church like this. I have only called you to follow me. My resurrection life will flow through you to the people. It is my church! Just be my instrument!" I opened my eyes again and this great church looked so small to me. I would have no problem preaching wherever God called me to preach because I was just an instrument in God's hands. This understanding has remained with me all these years. Whether I am speaking to four people in a small group or I am preaching on a golf course in Shillong, India to 60,000 people, I am only an instrument in God's hands. My prayer is that you would be obedient to the leading of the Holy Spirit. Be an instrument in God's hands. They are incredible hands that hold the whole world! Let Him take your hand and resurrection life will explode within you and you will be filled with joy. When Jesus shows up, peace fills our soul.

*"Therefore encourage one another and build each other up,
just as in fact you are doing."*
I Thessalonians 5:11

Chapter 6

The Beloved Mentor

To tell our story without recognizing the impact that Dr. David Grubbs had on both Judy and me would be like omitting a key ingredient from a recipe. As we sought to grow as Christians, we quickly realized that the pastor of our home church was at best a baby believer like us. Finding little or no help in answering our questions in our church, we sought out Dr. Grubbs, the Senior Pastor of Salem Ave. Church of God in Dayton, Ohio. We now recognize that our relationship with Dr. Grubbs was being orchestrated by the Lord. He warmly befriended and encouraged us. Much to our surprise, he also challenged us to stay in the United Methodist church we had been attending. He felt that we could be a light to help the church grow and to help them reach other people for Christ.

Many possibilities for discipleship and training were available at Salem Ave. Church. Dr. Grubbs made the church's resources available to us, and we got involved quickly. Our new walk with Christ was thrilling and we could not get enough of the gospel. We attended a class for new Christians and Judy joined the Evangelism Explosion program. Since our home church had no Sunday evening services or training classes, we began to attend Salem on Sunday nights. Dr. Grubbs was a powerful preacher and we grew greatly under his ministry of the Word of God. It was while listening to Dr. Grubbs that I began to understand that he was anointed by the Holy Spirit. Our hearts would be strangely warmed by his preaching and teaching. Our hunger for more of the Word of God grew and grew.

Dr. Grubbs was always available to us and was pushing us out of our comfortable nest to expand our influence for the Lord. He arranged for me to share my testimony at the International Camp Meeting of the Church of God in Anderson, Indiana. Thousands gathered each June for this event. He was always stretching us and challenging us beyond our own ability. This fostered a huge dependency on the Holy Spirit.

When Dr. Grubbs asked us to consider being baptized by immersion, we realized that our infant baptism did not meet the criteria found in Scripture. Biblical baptisms were usually individuals who believed. Although some new Christians were baptized as a family, infants are usually not yet believers. With this understanding, we agreed to be baptized by immersion. Taking this step made us more aware that our old life was buried with Christ and our new life had begun. What we thought was a simple step of obedience brought about some family conflict. Both families reiterated that they were absolutely sure our infant baptisms were totally sufficient. For this reason, both of our families boycotted the Sunday evening baptism.

Antioch is changed

As we continued to attend Antioch United Methodist Church, God began to do a powerful work among the people. The catalyst was the Campus Crusade for Christ Lay Institute for Evangelism. Fourteen of us had attended the event and all 14 came back excited about their faith, most as brand new believers. Even our pastor ended up attending the Lay Institute and God really touched him.

Although I taught an adult Sunday School class prior to the conference, I now understood that I had been devoid of spiritual life. We were using a denominational teaching guide for the class. Any time the material would mention the Holy Spirit, I would skip it. I had no idea what this term meant nor did anyone else in the class. After the conference, people in the Sunday School class heard the testimonies of those who had gone to the Lay Institute. Many in the class began accepting Christ as their Savior. We started a class for new Christians led by the pastor and began a visitation program where we visited every family on the church role in order to share the gospel. A prayer meeting was started on Wednesday evenings to intercede for the needs and ministries in the church and to study the Word of God. For us, this group became a new family. We were so excited to share life with them. This was our first taste of true Christian fellowship and the love of God was transforming us all.

As might be expected, when a major change is made in the church, there is often resistance by some of the members. Even so, our church of 70 grew rapidly until a particular morning when 200 people attended. This was one of the most exciting worship experiences our church had ever enjoyed. John Lynch, our wonderful mentor from Campus Crusade, shared his testimony and the *Four Spiritual Laws* with all the people in attendance. Many people had life-changing experiences that morning as they made decisions for Christ. I remember that Sunday morning well because a United Methodist Bishop was attending. Although he differed in doctrine with the Calvinism he had heard, he stated, "At least something is happening here." He was contrasting our lively church to many of the dead churches for which he was overseer.

As new believers, one of our problems was that we knew little about spiritual warfare. When the pastor started having altar calls on Sunday mornings, some of the longtime members of the church met with him and ordered him to stop. They also told him to cease the efforts to visit all church members because some had voiced complaints. When he continued altar calls, many of these same people expressed their displeasure by getting up and walking out of the service. Their caustic behavior was obvious to all. They also disapproved of the mid-week prayer meeting. One man confronted me in the parking lot on Sunday morning right after the worship service. He said, "You need to stop these (**&^^%$$#*#%&) prayer meetings and Bible studies. We want our church back like it was." Great pressure was put on the pastor, even to the point of threatening his employment.

Finally, one Sunday morning, he stood in the pulpit and apologized to all who had been offended. He said all altar calls and visitation being done by church members would stop. Many of us who were new believers felt like we had been ostracized because of our commitment to Christ and had been betrayed by our pastor. There was a mass exodus of these young believers from the church. This was a very difficult situation for Judy and me. This was the church of my youth and our family church; we had a long history with this church. David Grubbs was still telling us we were in a fertile evangelism field, so we should stay. However, we were concerned that our girls would not meet Jesus in a church that had basically just asked Him to leave. We finally decided to leave Antioch while making a transition from my engineering career to seminary at Anderson School of Theology.

Thus, began our pilgrimage into the Church of God and we became part of Salem Avenue Church. This was the place where we first heard the gospel, where we were baptized, where we were called to ministry, where our girls found Christ, where I preached my first sermon, where I was ordained, where I had my first staff position as Director of Evangelism and Discipleship, where I did my first wedding and my first funeral, all under the mentoring of Dr. Grubbs.

When I first began to understand the doctrine of this new church, I realized how well it fit our personal beliefs. It was wonderful to see all races and cultures mixing in the Lay Ministry of Campus Crusade. In the Church of God, a major value was the unity of all born-again believers. We would often hear this in teaching and it was so refreshing to see it lived out in our church. It was frequently stated that this was a church where Christian experience made you a member, not rote confirmations and membership ceremonies. We knew that the way anyone became a member of Christ's church was to be born again. There was also an emphasis on a holy lifestyle. Integrity was expected from a believer in relationship to God and with each other. These tenets of faith were believed and practiced at Salem.

Not only was Dr. Grubbs a great teacher and mentor, but he taught us to serve. Our church reached out to other churches and held Evangelism and Discipleship Clinics. Dr. Grubbs would scholarship many pastors who couldn't afford the registration fee. We helped in these conferences. On one occasion, Dr. Grubbs bought me a suit demonstrating to us his benevolent heart. (A major motivation may also have been his dislike of some of my suits, but I prefer to believe the former reason.)

Our discipleship ministry was enhanced by the launching of a small group ministry where Judy and I met weekly with seven couples for about a year. They were recruited through prayer and because we believed they had the potential to be great Growth Group leaders. All of us were greatly motivated and very passionate about this ministry. It is hard for me to describe the depth of connection we had in this group. We experienced some of what Heaven is going to be like. Some of these people remain good friends to this day. After about a year together, we launched seven small groups with 10-12 in each group. These groups became care centers and outreach centers at Salem.

Some of these Growth Group leaders were relatively new Christians. Because of this, there was a great hunger for the Lord. Chapter 7 is the story of one of these couples, Jody and Linda McGuire. Another Growth Group leader couple was David and Marilyn McQuinn. They had been involved in their pre-Christian days in some satanic rituals, hoping to find God. They had seen the power of Satan demonstrated. During this time of searching, David was reading the book *Late Great Planet Earth* written by Hal Lindsey. God convicted him that he wasn't ready for the impending judgment of God. God really spoke to his heart in this book, and he accepted the Lord. Soon after that, Marilyn was at the altar of the church asking Christ into her life. Their hunger for God had led them in their spiritual search through the darkness of Satan's deception to the light of new life in Christ. Other members of this first group were Doug and Jan Scherer, Dave and Ginny Green, Chuck and Janet Smith and Mike and Connie Payne.

I had challenged David McQuinn to lead a New Christian Class since he and Marilyn were such good role models. He was open to the idea but reminded me that he was a smoker and wondered how that would effect his teaching, leading, role model, etc. He had tried to quit smoking but was really struggling. David and I prayed about the need for deliverance. As we were praying, I saw a picture that was an answer to our prayer. It was a man sitting in a dark room wishing for a light to be turned on. He was just crying out to the light, "Turn on, turn on!" A friend finally suggested that the man walk across the room and flip the light switch. When he flipped the light switch, the room was filled with light. I am not one to have visions like this very often. David was the man in the room. He was asking God for a miracle to deliver him from smoking. All he needed to do was flip the switch, exercise his will, and God would give the victory. David made a choice not to smoke, he quit, and God gave him victory. He and Marilyn have had a powerful impact for the Kingdom and still do to this day.

In another area of my church responsibility, we had about 150 people involved in the weekly evangelistic visitation program. Our church became a training center for Evangelism Explosion and to this day many Church of God pastors point back to these training sessions as life-changing experiences. I remember one training session where there were pastors and lay people from about 40 different church backgrounds, all meeting together to learn how to more effectively share their faith. Our trainers were lay people who each took two trainees out to make evangelistic home visits. Typically, 15 or twenty people received Christ in these training visits. I believe God opened the eyes of many leaders and showed them what equipped and gifted lay persons can do to advance the gospel. I believe God said, "Well done," every time we trained pastors and lay people from other churches. This was always a growing time for our lay leaders. It strengthened them in the Lord as they realized their ministry went far beyond our local church. They were training pastors to effectively train other lay people to be witnesses to the light.

This wonderful church gave us a great foundation and grew from 500 to 1000 in the four years we were involved. Much of this was evangelistic growth, meaning the church was growing by non-Christians accepting the Lord. Jesus showed up at Salem and the whole North Dayton area was impacted. It was a honeymoon experience that shaped us and prepared us for what was to come. Judy had many doubts about whether she wanted to be a pastor's wife, but the love and support of this congregation brought great healing and hope to her. Dr. Grubbs has since gone to be with the Lord. We miss him greatly and are so indebted to him for the countless hours he poured into our lives. He showed us what a life looks like when Jesus shows up!

"My message and my preaching were not with wise and persuasive words, but with a demonstration of the Spirit's power, so that your faith might not rest on men's wisdom, but on God's power." I Corinthians 2:4

Chapter 7

The Scholar and the Gospel

Matthew 22:14 states, "Many are called, but few are chosen." One such man who was both chosen and called is Jody McGuire. He represented one of the greatest stories of transformation that I have personally experienced.

Jody's wife Linda visited Salem Ave. Church of God one Sunday morning. I was training Marty Grubbs, a high school student enrolled in our Evangelism Explosion program. He was the son of Dr. David Grubbs whom I talked about in Chapter 6. Our Thursday evening visitation packet had Linda's name as a newcomer. Linda was the daughter of Marvin Mitchell, a weekly worshipper at Salem Avenue Church of God. He had prayed for and witnessed to Linda and her husband Jody for many years. He had planted many good seeds in their lives. Marty and I made our way to the McGuire's house to follow-up on Linda's visit. Linda greeted us warmly at the door and invited us into their home. Jody was not home; he was out playing tennis. While waiting for Jody's return, I noticed that he had extensive library of philosophical works. Right in the center of the book shelf was the book *God is Dead* by Niche. The thought crossed my mind that if Jody had read all of these books, we might be in for a challenging evening. That thought was truly prophetic.

When Jody finally arrived, he was very courteous. We learned quickly that he was a deep thinker. He asked difficult theological and philosophical questions, some of which I wished I had the answers to myself. As we tried to share the gospel with Jody, we had to deal with many objections: "What about all the good people who have never heard the gospel? Are they going to hell because they don't worship a Jesus of whom they have never heard? If God is so loving, why does he let sin run rampant in the world?" We had a very exhausting, thoughtful and difficult discussion. Marty and I both felt as if we were in a wrestling match, and in some ways we felt overmatched. Jody was a well-educated, well-read and brilliant young man.

As I tried to answer Jody's questions, my young high school trainee, Marty, later told me he was thinking to himself, "I never want to have to answer questions like these." Currently, Marty pastors Crossings Community Church in Oklahoma City, Oklahoma, one of the largest churches in the Church of God movement, where he undoubtedly has had to deal with many such questions during his long tenure in ministry. I know Marty's prayers made a difference as I shared the gospel with Jody.

All of my best efforts to simply share with Jody what Christ had done for me just produced more questions, some of which were unanswerable. Finally, after about two hours of this mental and emotional stress, it was time to leave. It was going to be a relief to get into the car and escape this mentally taxing episode. Our minds and emotions were definitely in need of refreshing. Being worn out from the debate, I remember breathing a prayer, something like "Help!" as I walked toward the door.

It was then that I felt an inner prompting to ask Jody if he was genuinely seeking the truth. He pointed at all his books and assured me he was definitely seeking the truth. I replied that if he were really seeking truth, he would ultimately find it in Christ who is the Truth. He then stated that he could not deny our personal stories about how Christ had impacted our own lives, but he said it wasn't for him. I asked him if he was willing to read a book written by C. S. Lewis entitled, *Mere Christianity*. He said he would, so I sent the book to him the next day. This book was used greatly by God in my life to answer many questions that helped my faith journey. I was hoping it would do the same for Jody.

Sometime later, Jody came into Salem Avenue Church looking for me or Dr. Grubbs. He found Dr. Grubbs is his office. Jody walked into the office, threw the *Mere Christianity* book on his desk and said that the book had destroyed his belief system. This gesture proved to be Jody's way of announcing that he was now a Christ-follower. Jody wanted reassurance that he had accepted Christ correctly. Dr. Grubbs helped him solidify his new decision and we all tried to encourage him greatly.

This brilliant new Christian started attending Salem regularly. One Sunday morning while sitting in the balcony of the church, he heard God calling him to ministry. Jody had nearly completed a Doctorate in Earth Sciences and he was currently teaching in a

Catholic high school. When God called him, He began shaking Jody's whole world and it was a frightening moment for him.

In response to this sense of call, Jody got up from his seat and left the service. He jumped into his car and literally tried to escape. He didn't drive far when he realized he couldn't outrun God so he pulled his car off the road and surrendered his life totally to the Lord. Thus began a fantastic journey for Jody and Linda.

I have no idea how many people have come to Christ because of the witness of Jody and Linda McGuire. Jody had a teaching ministry for over 30 years at Salem Avenue Church. He became a highly valued staff member. In the early days of his decision to follow Christ, Jody was able to leverage his Catholic background and get into schools where he was a powerful witness for Christ. He helped me in a ministry to drug addicts in Brookville, Ohio, and was able to influence many to become Christ-followers. Jody also became a Yokefellow, a discipleship group of bright thinkers started by Elton Trueblood at Earlham College. Elton was always looking for brilliant young scholars to develop fully as Kingdom people. Jody's association with this group of disciples caused him to grow rapidly in the Lord.

Linda was also used by God in many ways and was a wonderful partner to Jody in each step they took in ministry. She started a Christian School at Salem and developed it into a wonderful ministry. She has been and still is a bold and faithful witness to Jesus Christ.

A few years later, we would meet Linda's brother and sister-in-law when they visited the church we were pastoring in Dallas, Texas. We were privileged to see both Greg and Laura make decisions for Christ and to have their lives transformed by the power of the gospel. In the same way that Jody and Linda became involved at Salem Avenue Church, Greg and Laura quickly became very involved in the ministry of the Dallas First Church of God.

God has continued to weave our lives into the family of Jody and Linda McGuire although geographically we have not been close since the 1970s. This story went full circle when Judy and I were visiting the Dayton area and attended a new church plant called New Covenant Church in Vandalia, Ohio. Jody was the founding pastor of this church plant. As we sat under his gifted teaching, my mind went back to my first visit with Jody. God's marvelous power to change lives had made it possible for both Jody and Linda to greatly impact people in the Dayton area through their ministry. My prayer is that God will continue to be glorified through the lives of the McGuires and that their family will demonstrate the greatness of our God. Thank you, God, for friends who will be "forever friends" because we will share eternity in Heaven together. The richest parts of our lives come from spending time with our brothers and sisters in Christ.

As Christians, the miraculous life of Christ is in us. It is not unusual for us to see miracles. Of all the miracles of God, the power of a transformed life is the most impressive to me. I have seen God heal, deliver and set people free from the clutches of Satan, but the greatest miracles of all are the ones that transform the heart and mind of a John and Judy Boedeker or a Jody and Linda McGuire. Our changed lives are our testimony to Jesus showing up! Glory to God!

"The weapons we fight with are not the weapons of the world. On the contrary, they have divine power to demolish strongholds." II Corinthians 10:4

Chapter 8
Battle with the Mafia

As I previously stated, there was a time when we tried to sell our country home and couldn't understand why it didn't sell. God had other plans for this house. God used this property to change a community. Our small rural town of Brookville, Ohio appeared to be a small sleepy village. It was thought to be a safe environment. It was quiet, and it rolled up its sidewalks early in the evening. We had no idea that our local Main Street, with many old family businesses, came to life at night with a very different culture. Brookville had a very sinister drug trade that was supplying much of the Dayton area with drugs. Most of us knew little or nothing about this underworld. Alcohol was my drug of choice before I became a Christian. I knew nothing about other drug usage, but my naivety would soon end.

One Monday morning, Dr. David Grubbs called Randy Rohr, the Youth Pastor at Salem, and me into his office to tell us a very intriguing story. He had received a call in the middle of the night from two young men, Randy and Doug, both in their late 20's. They asked for an early morning meeting with Dr. Grubbs. Randy had a long-term relationship with Salem as it was his family's church. As a young man in high school, he was a believer who had a close walk with Christ. One night at a party, he was given a dare by some of his peers to try drugs just once to see how it felt. To prove to them it would not effect him, he tried his first drug. Randy's body reacted to the drug instantly and he was soon addicted. This began years of drug use and led to heroin addiction. He became part of the Brookville underground drug culture. One of Randy's friends, Doug, was also deeply connected to the drug traffic in Brookville. He was a huge man about 6' 10", 260 pounds and a notorious brawler who broke people's arms for fun. This is no doubt why he seldom had anyone turn him down when he later invited them to a Bible study at our home.

The night Randy and Doug had contacted Pastor Grubbs, they had previously attended a party where they had become high on drugs. After leaving the party late at night, they decided to take a walk on the railroad track that dissects Brookville. While walking, they suddenly experienced "a Presence." It was frightening, but yet exhilarating. The frightening part was that they were suddenly stone-sober. The exhilarating part was a divine, supernatural visitation. Calling Dr. Grubbs was the result of their desire to understand what had happened to them. As a response to this night meeting, both Randy and Doug asked Christ into their lives. This divine appointment would eventually shake Brookville and the whole drug underworld.

Dr. Grubbs saw a great need for these two new believers to have someone who would be available to them to help answer their questions and to disciple them. He knew that without someone actively involved in their lives, the drug culture would quickly claim them again. Since I lived in the same town as Randy and Doug, I was asked to follow-up on them. Randy Rohr, the Youth Pastor of Salem, was also given the assignment to help disciple these two new converts. We both hoped to encourage them in their new walk with the Lord. After we called to make an appointment with them and to determine a good place to meet, we made our way into a neighborhood which we later learned was notorious for drug trafficking. Our destination was a house in downtown Brookville. We soon learned this was a gathering place for many of the drug users and drug mules—those who sold and supplied drugs. Randy Rohr and I knocked on the door and asked for Randy and Doug. They were not at the house, but their names opened the door for us. We entered feeling very out of place as the diabolical spirits in this smoke-filled room were eternally opposed to the Spirit we brought into the room. I was greatly apprehensive about being in this foreign setting. The smell of marijuana was obvious, even to someone who knew nothing about drugs. Several people did exit via the back door as we entered, fearing we were NARCS (drug agents).

After a time, Randy Rohr was invited to bring in his guitar and began playing some songs. I then asked the young people if I could share some good news with them. I told them in a conversational format what Christ had done for me. I was amazed that they allowed us to share with them. I was no sooner finished than one of our new friends got up and began to testify that drugs did everything for him that I said Jesus had done for me. The first battle in the drug wars had begun and there was no clear winner. We were totally unprepared for the sights, sounds, smells and reactions of this group.

Since Randy and Doug never came home, we went to another home and a bar which we were told they often frequented, but we did not find them. In one bar we visited, I did manage to provoke a young man to pour a beer over my head because I was talking to him about the Lord. This was the first "baptism" of the new ministry, but I never thought it would be a bottle of beer on my head! The following week, I called Randy again. He was remorseful about standing us up, so we made another appointment to see him and Doug. This time they kept their commitment and we had a good meeting with them. They still remembered the supernatural visitation and their prayers for Christ to come into their lives. I invited them to bring some of their friends to our house in the country for a barbeque. They told us they would definitely be there with some of their friends. We prepared food for 12 people, but no one showed up! We were beginning to learn that in the drug culture, time commitments mean almost nothing. This was frustrating for us because it felt like our attempts to build a relationship were being snubbed. Meanwhile, many were simply living for the next high. Life in the world of drugs passes by with little structure.

Once again, we called Randy and told him we had a lot of food that he and his friends didn't eat. We invited him to try it again. He seemed ashamed about standing us up again. This time Randy, Doug and 10 of their friends actually arrived at our house and they ate everything we put in front of them. This meeting launched an incredible adventure none of us will forget.

What transpired in the next two years was like living again in the book of Acts with great wonders and signs affirming the gospel. After attending one of our meetings, Dr. David Grubbs said, "This is more like the book of Acts than any ministry I have ever seen." Not only were the lives of many young people transformed, but our lives were changed as well as we experienced the power of God being released in miraculous ways.

We started a Tuesday night Bible Study that grew from the original 10 to an average of 70 each week. Nearly 70 young people accepted Christ in the next two years. Over 200 people were touched by this ministry in a short two-year span. Our basement became a place where God showed up with healings and miracles on a weekly basis. I remember baptizing 19 of these young people in one evening at Salem.

High School counselors from Brookville asked if they could attend our Bible study because they wanted to see how these hardened kids could change so much in such a short time. Our group of young Christians were continuously witnessing to the other students in Brookville.

It needs to be said that the human instruments that God used were absolutely unable to do this ministry apart from God's Spirit. Every week before the Bible study met, we who were leading got on our knees to plead with the Lord to show us what we needed to do. God was so faithful to do what we asked him to do. We prayed for knowledge on what to teach; He gave it! We prayed for musicians; He sent them! We asked God to bring salvation to these young people; He did it! We asked for favor with these young people, and the Lord gave it!

This was not an easy ministry. Satan does not give up his territory easily. The attacks against us were brutal. We were on a steep learning curve about the culture of drugs. Some visitors stole prescription drugs from our medicine cabinet. We made trips to emergency rooms with some who overdosed. We were in a real struggle for the lives of these young people. Once we were raided by local police who thought we must be selling drugs in order to get all these known drug users to come to our house. We also began to get threats from the Brookville underworld because certain drug lords' interests were being affected by our Bible study. The mules were no longer carrying drugs, and many young people were being delivered from their habits. Even with these victories, I did five funerals, all drug-related deaths, in two years for some who were in our ministry.

One funeral was for a man I will call Dank. He was a 260-pound biker who looked really mean. He died in a drug-related shooting but had given his heart to Christ before this happened. He had told me that he wanted to tell all his friends about Christ. On the day of the funeral, I heard a deafening sound that rocked the whole church. It was the arrival of all the Harleys in the Motorcycle Club in which Dank rode. They revved up their engines, drowning out every other noise in the area. This rough-looking group came in and took a row in the church but instead of sitting in the pew, they sat on top of the back of the seats. I shared with them the wonderful story of the gospel as Dank would have told it. Many were weeping at the end of the message and Dank's wish to get the gospel to his friends was answered. I felt the Lord's assurance that some of his friends accepted Christ.

Many well-meaning people lectured us about having our two young girls around all of these older kids who were involved in drugs. My girls "fell in love" with some of these young people. They saw the tearful episodes where kids who were high on drugs could not remember where they lived. They also saw heartsick parents who panicked over overdoses and hospital visits. Their first-hand observations of how drugs destroyed the lives of their friends gave them a great aversion to any form of drug.

Our home in the country was the center of this drug ministry. We had a small lake where our new friends could swim. We had a ping pong table and a small pool table which they enjoyed. We now knew without a doubt why our home didn't sell when we put it on the market. During our two-year involvement with these young people, challenges and opportunities came to us in many forms.

One day, a young man who looked like he had been mud wrestling rang our doorbell. We met a stranger by the name of Bill who was extremely depressed and wondered if he wanted to live. He was driving his car at a high rate of speed down Brookville-Pyrmont Pike, the road where we lived. He told us later that he had purposely driven off the road, trying to hit a tree to kill himself. He missed the tree and got stuck in mud. He came knocking on our door covered with mud and filled with great anxiety and depression. We had an opportunity to pray with Bill and Christ invaded his life as his Healer. His sister, Sherry, would soon come to Christ, also.

Years later, I was the evangelist for a Camp Meeting in Alabama. After preaching in the evening service, I was walking back to my cabin in the dark and someone jumped on my back, scaring me to death. It was our friend Bill. He was now an Elder in a church in Alabama and was following the Lord along with his family. To see Bill following Christ with passion and vigor years after Christ became real to him brought an explosion of joy to my life. Over the years God has been gracious to again bring us across the paths of some of the most troubled young people who had been part of our Bible study. Some of these now have an abundant, fulfilling life in Christ.

Sara* came to our Bible study for the first time. She was deeply involved in witchcraft and told us that her mom was a Wicca witch. Yet Sara had a hunger for God and eventually she came to Christ. Believers prayed for Sara and she was wonderfully delivered from her demonic past. Not long after this, I heard our door bell ring and went to answer it. At the front door was Sara's mother telling me to take my $#@@$%^^*&%$#@@$ gospel and leave her daughter alone. She literally screamed at me saying that she would rather have her daughter on drugs any time than to be involved with Jesus Christ. She left, but Sara was determined to keep following the Lord. There were always surprises and unexpected opportunities and challenges like these showing up at our front door during these exciting days of ministry.

Another incident involved Adam*, a man who drove his van up our long driveway and knocked on our door. He was convinced we were drug dealers because many of his drug-using friends came to our house. He wanted drugs, but instead I offered him Jesus Christ. He made it clear he didn't want Jesus. He said, "I have a van, my motorcycle, a sharp chick in Malibu, California who I am going to see. You don't have anything I want or need." I heard several weeks later he was shot and killed in a drug bust. It broke my heart every time we lost one of these young people because they were precious to God, made in His image. I did have something he desperately needed. Jesus had offered him the gift of eternal life, but he was too blind to receive it.

As we prayed for the destruction of the drug culture in our area, God seemed to make things known which would advance our cause. Randy Rohr and I received a tip about where one of the top drug lords lived in the Dayton area. He was the number one kingpin who supplied most of the drugs in our area. We decided he needed a personal visit, so we proceeded to make a house call. Both Randy and I prayed with more urgency the closer we got to his house. We were scared and feeling great anxiety on this drive. I remember thinking, "John this is the most stupid thing you have ever done." Without the prayer, we would have turned around, but an unseen Power led us. The man lived out in the country outside of Dayton. As we pulled up to his house, we noticed the fenced yard with "vicious dog" warning signs everywhere. The Dobermans, Rottweilers and Pit Bulls in the yard looked like ravenous sharks. We sounded the horn to no avail. Probably evidencing more zeal than wisdom, Randy and I prayed for God to shut the mouths of the dogs just as he shut the mouths of the lions to protect Daniel. We opened the gate, entered the yard and walked up to the house, not looking right or left for fear of seeing a charging dog. The dogs acted almost as if they couldn't see us. I wonder...?

The man's wife answered the door. She called her husband and he and his wife sat at the table with us for over an hour. This man knew exactly who we were. I strongly suspect that some of the threats we had received were from him. We explained why we were involved with the Brookville kids and what we were doing. We also told him that we felt God had prompted us to come and talk to him and his family because He wanted us to share His love with him. After a time, this "tough" man ended up in tears. He told us he wished he could change for the sake of his family, but he made a six-figure salary and had no education to enable him to support his family by any other means. His wife was interested in praying with us, but when her husband declined our invitation to receive Christ, she also decided against asking Christ into her life at that time. I hope the Word penetrated their hearts because a couple weeks later this man was killed in a drug incident. As we departed, the dogs again seemed totally unaware of our presence!

During the period that I was involved in this drug ministry, I kept a journal. The following are a few journal entries from 1974-1975 that give a sense of what was happening through the Holy Spirit. To be sensitive to privacy, last names are eliminated.

1. October 28, 1974: Happy Birthday, John. Bible study at Ron and Sandi's house.
   Attendees: Chris, Bob, Marilyn, Mike, Connie, Jim, Amy, Randy, Joanne, Caroline, Gordon and Jocelyn.

Praise the Lord for birthday parties that lead to spiritual birthdays!

2. December 23, 1974: 44 at Bible Study. Mike received Christ.
3. January 8, 1975: Toby prayed to receive Christ; 19 years old and deeply into drugs.
4. January 19, 1975: Dave prayed to receive Christ. Baptized Teresa, Diana, Toby, Mike, Sherry, Sheila, Joe, Dawn.
5. January 26, 1975: Gave their heart to Christ: Kim, Monica, Joe, Pam, Mary, Joe, Mike, Donna.
6. February 3. 1975: 77 in attendance, Craig prayed to receive Christ, Peggy and Donna also accepted the Lord.

These are just a few of the excerpts from my journal. I am deeply indebted to Joanne Kuch for being a major contributor to this ministry. Her love deeply touched many of these kids. She opened her home night and day; she was always available to talk to anyone at anytime. Long before we became involved in this effort, she started opening her home every Friday evening for these kids. She is now receiving her reward in Heaven. Jody McGuire and Randy Rohr were deeply involved also. They prayed, they taught, and Randy played guitar. I appreciated our band of Sonny McGrath and the Smith brothers, gifted musicians who lead us in Scripture songs. God sent them to us at a time they were greatly needed.

I loved the fact that some of our new converts were growing so rapidly that they became leaders of breakout groups during our Bible studies. I also was thankful that some of the parents of these teens got involved with us in ministry to these needy kids.

A good question is why this group of young people from ages 16-30 got entwined in heavy drug dependency. In a study I made while at seminary, and after many interviews with parents and young people, I concluded that most were there because their parents stopped fighting for them. Some parents had tried to intervene and had just gotten tired trying. Others had never been involved in their kid's lives so there were no boundaries. A very small number rebelled against very strict controls by their parents. A few came from stable homes but became addicted to their drug of choice. The majority by far were being destroyed because there were no boundaries established to protect them in their home and family.

To this day, I am still meeting people who were touched and blessed by this special move of God in 1974 and 1975. God did far beyond what any of us expected. He transformed both a school and a town by His grace!

What happened to Randy and Doug, the two young men who started this story? Randy lived with us for about 6 months, but it took about two years before he was totally set free from drugs. During the time Randy lived with us, there was a contract out on his life because he owed the drug dealers a lot of money. Judy gave him her paycheck and took Randy to the place where his bills needed to be paid. She remarked that for several weeks she was on pins and needles about who was going to show up to harm Randy and possibly us. The day they delivered the money, I was out of town, so Judy and Randy went alone. This was a very frightening thing for Judy to do. Randy would not let Judy enter the house where the contact to pay off the debt was made. She sat in the car on the dimly lit street hoping against hope that she would not hear a shot. Randy soon returned in one-piece rejoicing that his debt had been paid.

As stated earlier, we moved Randy into our home to help him and to protect him from himself and bad influences. He was doing well for six months until, unfortunately, we went on vacation and some old friends found Randy and tempted him. As he had done many times in his life, Randy made a bad choice. His relationship with Christ was an on-again off-again experience. He knew the truth. He had accepted Christ, but his walk was not consistent. Later, Randy ended up living in Dallas where we were called to pastor. He was still making bad choices. Then, since he lived far away from our South Dallas church, he got involved in Word of Faith Church in North Dallas. One day while taking a shower, he began to speak in tongues and he was immediately set free of drug dependence. Randy now serves the Lord because God supernaturally transformed his life. God has a good sense of humor. This particular church was led by a man whom only God can judge, but to me he was a charlatan. I do not come from a Pentecostal background, so I certainly did not teach Randy about the gift of tongues. I do know by Randy's testimony that from that special moment in the shower to my last contact with him, he has been free of drugs.

Doug had an untimely death through a car accident. Only God can judge Doug's spiritual condition at his death. I trust that God's grace opened a way for him and that he has preceded us to Heaven. His girlfriend, Chris, who was unhappy when Doug became a Christian, is now a committed Christian herself and she has her children in a Christian school. It will be wonderful to see this great cloud of witnesses, including at least 70 plus young people from the Brookville area, praising Christ in Heaven.

One final comment about Doug: Because of him, my faith in God's power to transform a life increased greatly. This "bad dude" was feared by the whole city of Brookville. His ability to subdue even the meanest of the Brookville gang was legendary. To see him humbled and in tears, thanking God for his salvation was incredible. I also had the joy of baptizing Doug. However, I made a strategic error in that I did not stand far enough behind him to compensate for his 6'10" height. As I tried to lay him back into the water, I went right in on top of him, making it the third time I had been baptized! If I count the baptism by beer, it is four! It gave us all a great laugh. I am trusting Doug is in the presence of the Lord as I share his story. When Jesus showed up to meet Randy and Doug as they walked along the railroad tracks outside of a small rural town named Brookville, He launched a powerful visitation of His Spirit over the entire area. We are so privileged to tell the story!

"And on this rock I will build my church, and the gates of Hades will not overcome it." Matthew 16:18

Chapter 9

Cowboy Boots and the Gospel

Even though Salem Avenue Church of God in Dayton, Ohio seemed like a wonderful oasis to us, restlessness was growing stronger to develop my own preaching ministry. God was stirring within my heart a desire to give away the grace He was giving me. I had opportunities to preach at times when Dr. Grubbs was absent and I also filled a few other pulpits for pastors who were vacationing. The more I preached, the more I understood that the major gifting of my life was to be an encourager for the body of Christ. I knew that I was to be an evangelistic voice for the Lord.

In 1977, I was contacted by the Pulpit Committee of First Church of God in Dallas, Texas. Judy and I had never lived anywhere except Ohio. Several months earlier, Judy casually shared with me that she felt like the Lord was showing her that we would live in the southwestern part of the USA. We had little exposure to this part of the country, so when we were contacted by the church in Dallas, it did not escape me that we were seeing the fulfillment of Judy's prophetic word. The prospect of a move to Texas was exciting, but it also meant leaving our families and life long friends in Ohio.

The Pulpit Committee invited us to visit the Dallas church in February of 1977 to candidate as the potential Senior Pastor. Even as we prepared to visit the church for a weekend, my heart was being drawn to Dallas. As we arrived, this confirmation grew as we met with various groups in the church and finally with the entire congregation.

Our hosts for this weekend were Orman and Juanita Baker. I realized the first time I met this couple that they were very special. Juanita was the church librarian and was always working to make the library function more effectively. She used the books and tapes to challenge people to grow and to give the tapes to others. I later realized that my messages went all the way around the world because of her diligence. Orman was an elder and Bible teacher extraordinaire. He taught the Bible in Sunday School and taught a Bible course in the public school for years. I have said before that this was one of the most committed lay couples I have ever pastored. Obviously, they gave us a very good first impression of the church.

To the west of Dallas, there is a large flat area known as Grand Prairie. It has a beautiful daytime view as you drive west on I-20. You can see far across the plains that at one time contained buffalo. At night, this same drive is a breathtaking view of thousands of points of light, each point being another home. As we drove west on I-20 on Saturday evening, we saw this beautiful sight. Immediately, God put a burden in my heart to get the good news of Christ to every point of light that we saw. It was a holy and hushed moment when with a tear in my eye, I agreed with God that this was my calling. Judy also believed that Dallas was our next home.

Our last event was the Sunday morning service where I shared the Word of God. Even though a candidate's sermon is a little artificial, a special anointing on the message touched everyone's heart. A vote was scheduled that evening to call me as their pastor. Judy and I went house hunting that Sunday afternoon and signed a letter of intent to buy a home even before the church had officially called me as their pastor. I remember telling Judy, "I am so sure that I am to be in Dallas that if First Church of God doesn't call us, there is another ministry here for us." Thankfully, though, I was called to be the pastor.

Jesus had shown up in the prophetic word about living in the Southwest. He had shown up in the vision of the lights in Grand Prairie and He had shown up to touch the hearts of the people at the First Church of God, confirming that I would be their new pastor. He also showed up in the miraculous way we sold our country home. We sold it "by owner" in the dead of winter, with snow covering much of our beautiful landscaping. The family who bought our much-loved property did so even though there were some obstacles. As they toured our home, our older daughter, Lynelle, accidentally set fire to our trash can, filling the kitchen and living room with smoke. Almost simultaneously, our dog Jingles nipped their child who was running across the field. This took some doctoring and some encouragement from his parents. They still bought the house at our full asking price! As our final day in Brookville dawned, we still had a baby grand piano and a 20 HP

Allis Chalmers tractor to sell. By day's end, we sold both of them for our asking price. God is never late!!

As we arrived in Dallas, our new home was still under construction. Dick and Shirley Rudman graciously invited us to stay in their home until our home was finished. We had a wonderful three weeks with this godly couple who remain some of our best friends to this day. We recently traveled to Kingsland, Texas to celebrate their 60th anniversary. We had a fantastic time sharing stories.

As a new pastor, I no longer had the problem of not having a place to preach. Instead, I had the challenge of preparing a message for Sunday mornings, Sunday evenings, and Wednesday evenings. The heavy preaching and teaching responsibilities drove me to prayer and long hours of study. All the way through this learning process, I felt the inspiration and the leading of the Holy Spirit.

Having never been the lead pastor with a church staff, I asked the Lord for certain people who could help us do the ministry. In particular, I asked for two people who could be trained in Evangelism Explosion ministry, two people who could be trained to lead a Small Group ministry and someone who could teach a New Christian Class. If God would provide these people, I was convinced He would then build His church through them. We were thrilled when these people came forward to take on these roles. Carl and Mary Williams became leaders of our Discovery Class for new Christians. Chuck Maze, Shirley Rudman, Susan Jones and Mary Williams became the first trainees in Evangelism Explosion. Our Associate Pastor, Wayne Putman, was at the church long before Judy and I knew it existed. He was also trained in Evangelism Explosion and was the spark for much growth in our church from both his youth ministry and his worship leadership. John and Linda Bloom stepped forward to lead our Small Group Ministry. God built His church through these committed people. We had a great leadership team and a church with committed people who were willing to follow godly leadership. God helped me see that a church of 110 people would not grow rapidly overnight. The church had little experience reaching out to their community. Getting back to the call of Jesus to "Go into the entire world" would take some effort. God showed me that new life would initially come like a slow trickle. Eventually, the trickles would form small streams. In God's timing, they would become moving rivers. The church would then become like a thundering rapids that would transform lives. This life-giving water was a rush of grace that would bring the gospel of healing and hope to our community and the world beyond.

The Dallas church began to be a life saving station. God's life was flowing through our people to others. Eventually the Evangelism Explosion ministry grew to about 50 people who went out weekly into the community to share God's love. The Small Group ministry grew from one initial group to 15 groups with over 150 people involved. We started a new six-week Discovery Class for new Christians every month to meet the needs of those coming to Christ. Part of God's provision for us was Henry Schnieder, a consultant from Churches Alive. He was a very wise counselor and was instrumental in keeping us on track. His help enabled us to start Sharing Clinics where we invited other churches in our community or in our movement to spend a few days with us in order to experience our discipleship ministries. This became a great growth point for our people because they could see that God was using their ministries to expand His kingdom over our entire country.

I remember one Evangelism Clinic where we had 19 participating churches with 40 trainees involved. On our last night together, we went out in groups of three into the community to share our faith. Twenty-six people made professions of faith in Christ that evening. We returned to the church with much joy. At the end of our meeting, we joined hands in a prayer circle that included Lutherans, Baptists, Methodists, Presbyterians, and a Catholic Priest. People from the Assembly of God, Church of God, and some Bible churches were also with us. As a final act of worship, we thanked God for what He had done that evening. As we celebrated, Heaven came down to earth. We all realized we were in the presence of the Lord. He was blessing us because we were expressing the beauty of being one in Christ. I believe He was also pleased with our desire to be used in reaching others with the gospel of Christ. This was a high moment of worship that none of us who stood in that circle will ever forget. When Jesus shows up, words cannot express the blessing.

Our youth and children's ministries became very effective due to the great leadership of pastors Wayne Putman and David Morales. We brought in Dennis Miller to coach Wayne and David and he had a great impact on helping us become more excellent leaders. His book *Changed Lives* was the book that brought structure and vision to our Jr. and Sr. High ministries. His leadership book also brought the scriptures alive in ways so that young people could understand who they are in Christ. I think this is why about 50 families from Wycliffe Bible Translators became part of our church. They wanted their missionary kids in a healthy church environment where they would be discipled with the Word.

Pastor Clay Houston, now deceased, was instrumental in developing a powerful College and Career ministry. His wife, Joy, was an important part of the leadership team. At its peak, over 70 young adults were part of this ministry and many lives were transformed by this outreach. Clay was a gifted teacher and theologian and astounded his professors at Southwestern Seminary by his creative mind and deep scriptural insights.

Pastor Bill Marshall and Pastor Bob Boyd were involved later but were vital leaders in evangelism and the church's teaching ministry. Both had a great heart for God and were quality staff persons. Bob was the Senior Pastor of Antioch United Methodist Church. This was the church of my youth. My mother was attending the church and she loved Bob's leadership and heart. We were honored greatly when he came to work with us on staff.

By God's grace, the church grew from 110 to an average of 550 persons. From 1977 to 1984, many lives were changed, and many people found hope and healing. There was a sense of unity and peace in our body as the church grew and prospered

The Korea Story, which I relate in Chapter 10, was a great part of what God used to bring revival to our church. We had a week long meeting in Mokpo, South Korea which was life-changing to Judy and me. Finally, the time came for us to go home to Texas. For a few days, we had stepped right into the pages of the book of Acts. I desperately wanted the power and zeal of the Korean church to be true of our Dallas First Church. We longed for our people to have the fire of God descend on them as it had on us. I felt that if Jesus was the same yesterday, today and forever as the scriptures say, then He could and would do the same things in Dallas that He was doing in Mokpo. We prayed for wisdom and sensitivity when we returned because people in our body had not experienced what we had experienced. I had been radically transformed in my understanding of praise, in my expectations of God to show up and demonstrate His power, and in understanding that prayer is the vehicle for God's supernatural visitation. Before going to Korea, I gave mental assent to the miraculous power of God, but we came home changed because we had seen it manifested.

When we returned from Korea, we made several changes in our ministry. One was to recruit prayer intercessors and begin a daily early morning prayer meeting. The second change was to begin to focus much more on praise music sung directly **to** God rather than testimony songs **about** God. I began to teach that praise was a spiritual weapon and the enemy did not like it. God began to move in revival in our church, and Satan began to do all he could do to stop it. We began seeing many miracles and were baptizing people almost every week.

The Revival

Revival came to our church as we prayed and praised. Our youth group caught on fire. Our students were meeting daily in the morning at the high school. They were praying for their fellow students and then witnessing to them during the day. We were doing two Sunday morning services and a Sunday evening Body Life service. Our Sunday night service was much more informal, and we could hold 350 in the sanctuary. It was filling up on Sunday evenings as people shared their victories, their defeats and their needs. God began to move powerfully in these sharing/prayer services. There was a sense of expectancy, wondering what God would do next. We opened our lives to one another and God was faithful to meet us.

The Conflict

We changed our worship style in 1983 before preparing our people for the change with teaching about worship. The change from testimony songs to direct praise to God was a battle for many churches especially the evangelical churches. When we began to have longer, unbroken times of praise, most people felt more able to express their love of God with clapping, with up-lifted hands, arms and hearts. For some of our people, this change took them out of their comfort zone. Some complained that they were embarrassed to bring their friends to our services because of these outward expressions. Some of our growth was coming from people looking for balance between sound teaching and powerful praise. Some came because they were in churches with praise but weak teaching. Some came because even though they had good teaching, their hearts desired an atmosphere of praise where God actually showed up. Some came through salvation and renewal.

A group of our own people was fearful that our worship style would lead us to become a full-blown charismatic church. This became a bigger issue when a visitor in our Sunday evening service spoke in tongues. It wasn't unusual for someone to quietly pray in tongues during a prayer time, but this was a message that could not be ignored. It was loud and focused everyone's attention on the speaker. Choosing to respond in a biblical manner, I waited for a minute or so and then asked for an interpretation. This did not come so I called the tongues out of order. This was the proof to some that we were becoming "Pentecostal." To some others, we quenched the Spirit. Several months after this infamous night, I learned that one of the matriarchs of our church had been given an interpretation but was afraid to share it because she knew some of her best friends did not believe in messages coming in the way this one had. The tongue, according to the interpreter, was a great message of encouragement and blessing from the Lord for our church and for our ministry. The teacher of our largest Sunday school class informed me the next morning that he and his family were leaving the church.

Part of the pain of this church conflict was that some of my best friends were in opposition to this new direction. In our eldership, eight elders were very supportive of our direction and two were not. These two were on the original Pulpit Committee that called me to the church. Since our bylaws called for unanimity in our leadership, we were paralyzed in dealing with these issues. These men went through a lot of the same trauma that our staff experienced. I owe so much to men who were willing to meet night after night to discern the difference between what God was doing and what the enemy was doing in the church. Thanks to Tom Hauser, Glen Bounds, Charlie Russell, Dick Rudman, Paul Reynolds, Ed Hickson, Tim Anstice, Harry May and Jim Keasler for their incredible service. Harry, Paul and Ed have gone to be with the Lord, but the impact they had continues.

Our staff was very supportive of the direction we were going, but even though we were in one accord, we had difficulty bringing the whole church to the same unity. After the Sunday night tongues episode, our elders put out a directive that we would allow no tongues speaking in our services. In retrospect, I now think this was an ill-conceived reaction to a one-time incident. I have often wondered if the Holy Spirit didn't leave that day because His manifestations were not welcome in our church. I had long had a desire to see evangelicals and charismatics walk together in unity. A good friend told me that if I walked down the middle of the road between these two groups, I would get hit by traffic from both directions. I picked up many wounds from this two-way traffic. However, this did not abolish the dream many of us had for a diverse body to be unified in Christ!

I will always be grateful for Wayne Putman, Bob Boyd, David Morales, Clay Houston, Bill Marshall and Alberta Hushfield for their support during these very difficult times. God used this team to push back the darkness and to advance the Kingdom of God. I was honored to serve with them.

The three-year period from 1984 to 1987 was a horrific time of my life. For Judy, it was even worse than it was for me. We were physically and emotionally exhausted. The burnout for me was not spiritual; emotionally it was extremely painful and unexpected. I was a cockeyed optimist and my "glass" was always half full, never half empty. A good friend, who was a counselor, diagnosed my depression. Pain and frustration were taking a toll on Judy and on me. There also had been terrible pressure on all of our leaders. There were outright attacks of the enemy both direct and through people. One night a dark suffocating spirit pinned me to my bed. I wasn't able to get free until Judy and I urgently called on the name of Jesus. Finally, an incredible peace filled the bedroom.

Anonymous calls were coming in the middle of the night calling me some names I had never heard. These rants were vicious and guttural. One Elder typed out 21 pages of charges that convinced him I should leave the ministry. Some people told Judy that they loved her, and their problem was only me. They followed this with a list of their complaints, wanting her to influence me. Denominational leaders were even contacted in hopes that their intervention could change our course. Fortunately, those who had complaints did not find the support they sought. The tremendous stress that I had experienced caused the loss of about 50% of my memory over this three-year period. The greatest pain of all was that I sensed we were losing the vision for the church. I remember screaming out to God, saying things like, "Where are You? Why don't You intervene? We are dying down here!" It was one of the two times since I became a Christian that I asked God to let me go back into my engineering career where I could just be a witness for Jesus and detach myself from church politics.

I also had my first experience with an oppressive spirit which felt like a heavy blanket over my head. It was a weight that I was not sure I could bear. I fasted and prayed, but it remained. I finally called three or four of our most committed intercessors to a meeting on Saturday morning. We all fasted and prayed and after about three hours of prayer the heavy spirit came off. I felt wonderful freedom and sensed an explosion of God's love and assurance. God taught me that when people are speaking ill against their own leadership, it will give the enemy the right to attack the leader. I am so thankful the blood of Jesus Christ was able to bring deliverance.

We then called a key leadership meeting in our church that I strongly requested Judy to attend. The proverbial straw that broke the camel's back was experienced by Judy. Some were expressing their disappointment with our staff. They felt we should have done more to calm the waters. Judy grabbed me and said, "Get me out of here; get me out of here; I can't take any more of this!" This was said through an open microphone within the hearing of all 75 church leaders. Juanita Baker and other loving people ushered Judy into my office to pray for her, and I met with our gracious elders who suggested that Judy and I leave town for a week of R&R.

When we returned from this retreat, the elders had arranged a four-month sabbatical for us. We spent the first two weeks at Marble Retreat in Colorado where Dr. Louis and Melissa McBurney had a unique ministry to pastors and missionaries. The time on the mountain was painful, but it yielded great breakthroughs in both of our lives. We always look back to Marble Retreat as a place where Jesus showed up and through the dedicated staff brought healing and restored hope. We then traveled some in Colorado and finally ended up in a mountain retreat in Montreat, North Carolina. We will always remember that Thanksgiving in Montreat when our two girls joined us, so we could process with them what we learned at Marble Retreat Center. This was a great time of tears, joy and breakthrough.

After coming back to the church, I shared with the congregation how much we needed them. We no longer were going to do ministry feeling so alone. There was a great outpouring of love and support from the church and we felt very encouraged. I had learned that Paul went through a similar situation that he shares in II Corinthians 1:8-11, "We do not want you to be uninformed brothers about the hardships we suffered in the province of Asia. We were under great pressure far beyond our ability to endure, so that we despaired even of life. Indeed, in our hearts we felt the sentence of death. But this happened that we might not rely on ourselves but on God, who raises the dead. He has delivered us from such a deadly peril, and he will deliver us. On Him we have set our hope that he will continue to deliver us, as you help us by your prayers." Paul had learned that he needed God's restorative power and the prayers of the saints to be healthy. Judy and I were well aware as never before of our need for complete dependency on God for healing and strength. If we were to continue our ministry in Dallas, we needed what Paul proclaimed in II Corinthians 12:10 "For when I am weak, then I am strong." We also needed the support of people in the congregation. It was time for the turmoil to end. The whole congregation had suffered long enough.

After those four months away and with help from a marvelous Christian psychiatrist, I was finally healthy enough to do something I should have done much earlier. I called the congregation to accountability and to a process wherein we could know how many people were willing to pursue our current direction. I was willing to stay in Dallas or leave if the congregation so desired. I preached about this vision on Sunday morning and then had a question and answer time on Sunday evening. After the Q and A period, we took a vote to determine what kind of support was in the congregation. Ninety-three percent of our people wanted us to keep our current direction. Seven percent did not. After the vote, I made it clear that the battle was over. No longer would we tolerate the resistance and paralysis. We were going to be moving forward and those who had resisted our direction needed to get on board or step aside. A small group of people decided they needed to step aside by leaving the church. They were part of planting another small church that to this day has only a handful of families. We wished them well after losing them to that new church plant and to other local churches. Thus, we began two years of peaceful ministry. I can honestly say we had neither ill will nor bitterness against any of the people who left. It is also true that it took several years for us to heal from the pain and hurt of this difficult period in our lives. I know our leaders also shared in the pain. The good news is that God used these experiences many times in our future ministry to help other pastors or churches.

While God was teaching and breaking us, He was doing a mighty work in the church. Not only had He grown the church from 110 to over 500, but wonders and signs followed as we prayed and praised. We had cried out to God, and He was building faith in our hearts. The following testimonies show some of the ways God worked. We called these "God sightings!" Only first names are used to protect people's privacy.

1. Ten-year old Kelly had a herniated navel. The way she expressed it, her belly button was an "outie,"not an "innie." As she grew older, kids would see the bump through her swimming suit and would ask questions. They would frequently push on it because it was a good target. One night Kelly decided that God could deal with this and she asked Him to give her an "innie" instead of an "outie." She proudly came out of the bedroom with a normal belly button.
2. Baby Garrett was born with a lump on his face. It disappeared after the laying on of hands and prayer.
3. Fred had a tumor requiring surgery. The church prayed for him. When the surgeon opened him up, there was nothing there.
4. Jack was in the hospital and was doing very poorly. He had a kind of Leukemia which would only respond to transfusions. Doctors finally told him that he could have no more transfusions. Judy woke up one night hearing a voice say, "I'm healing Jack." She didn't know what to do with this. Was this just a meaningless dream caused by her concern for the family? She went back to sleep and once again heard the voice. This happened three

times. The third time she heard the voice say, "I am healing Jack," she told me about it. The next day I visited Jack in the hospital. I joined in prayer with some of the family and his blood count returned to normal.
5. Phil had a terminal brain tumor. During prayer, intercessors saw a slow healing for Phil. Phil lived more than 20 years after these prayers.
6. Jeff had a blood disease that could be fatal. After a group laid hands on him and prayed for him, his blood returned to normal.
7. Colleen had issues in her marriage with anger. She and her husband had been in counseling for several years making little progress. A group of us gathered for prayer. After prayers for deliverance, she was set free from a demonic presence. The anger that controlled her has not returned.
8. Steve was a high school student who was having trouble understanding how to overcome darkness by the light of Christ. I met with him to discuss his relationship with the Lord. He really wanted a relationship with Christ and wanted to walk in God's plan for his life but was unable to respond to Christ's invitation to come into his life. I remember taking Steve to the point of salvation three or four times, and each time he said something like, "I want to but I can't." As intercessors prayed for this meeting and as I was trying to hear the voice of the Lord, I suddenly realized that I wasn't fighting Steve but was fighting Satan's power over him. I asked him if I could pray for him and I took authority in Jesus' name and commanded demonic powers to leave Steve. I prayed in the name of Jesus, in the

power of the cross and the power of the blood. After the prayer, Steve gladly asked Christ into his life. To God be the glory. By the way, Steve is the artist who did the cover of this book.

9. A man who had lived a double life for years as a worship pastor and as a practicing homosexual was delivered over the process of a couple years. One of the great celebrations in the life of our church came when he was married. He has had a wonderful ministry of life and hope to this day.

10. Judy had a sprained metatarsal arch which made it very painful to walk. A doctor had told her she would probably need surgery to fix it. Sitting at the back of the huge dome at Anderson Camp Meeting, a call for those needing healing was made. She asked God to heal her right where she sat. She walked out of the service with no pain and no limp and was completely healed.

11. Judy had a thyroid deficiency that required daily medication. One day she heard a message on the fact that we often hold on to illnesses because we just accept them as our norm. It had never occurred to her that God would or could heal her from something she never thought about. A strong impression came to her with the words, "This is for you" She stood and walked to the altar. The evangelist prayed for her and heat shot up and down her body. She went home and stopped all thyroid medication even though conventional wisdom would say not to do so until healing could be verified. She knew that she knew that she knew that she had been touched by God. God healed her and she lived without the medication for 35 years. She

did need a small dose in the last five years due to a parathyroid and thyroid surgery.
12. I had a herniated disc in my back because I was running with the wrong kind of shoes. Our elders anointed and prayed for me. Through their prayers and 10 days of bed rest ordered by my doctor, God healed the disc. However, this incident left a residual pain involving my left sciatic nerve. I suffered with it for many years. This pain made it difficult to sit for more than 10 minutes. While attending a conference where John Wimber was ministering, my sciatic nerve was screaming. John was receiving and speaking words of knowledge about healings. He spoke out about a sciatic pain that God wanted to heal, and described the problem with my sciatic. I must admit I was somewhat skeptical about this kind of healing ministry. But because of my pain, John's reputation and my belief in a healing God, I felt I needed to test it. I asked God if it was me that John Wimber spoke about. If so, He could heal me in my seat. As I put my hand on the sore area of the leg, I felt an explosion of heat go up and down my left leg and to this day I have never had another pain. I have not been nearly as skeptical about people ministering in a word of knowledge since that meeting.

After seeing God move in these powerful ways and personally experiencing these supernatural happenings, I am more convinced than ever that Jesus continues to touch people with his miraculous power on earth. I simply believe Jesus is exactly the same as when He lived on earth. It is exciting to know that He now lives in us. His ministry still saves the lost, delivers those in bondage and heals the sick. We need to trust Him and walk in His sufficiency. When Jesus shows up, miracles flow.

Our deep desire after coming back from South Korea was to see God's power released across the church in America. It was with that great longing in our heart for the power of God to be manifest that I went to preach in at a Camp Meeting in Western Canada. I had picked divine healing as my topic for a Wednesday night service. After the message, we prayed for the sick and an astounding thing happened. It appeared that everyone we prayed for was healed. One particular woman who was not able to walk came forward in a wheelchair. Her body shook continuously with palsy. As we prayed for this lady, we watched her shaking subside. After the meeting, she got up and started to walk. By the end of the week she was walking laps around the complex with no shaking.

Another person came forward and told us that she had suffered many years with horrible back pain. She used a TENS Unit to try to control pain. Sleep was impossible without it. She was anointed and prayed for that night. Immediately she felt relief from the pain and did not use her TENS Unit that night. She slept like a baby. By the end of the Camp Meeting she was totally free of pain. There were many testimonies of other healings during this Camp Meeting. God had moved mightily and many were healed. An interesting side note to this is that a week after these healings in Canada, I was preaching at the Wisconsin State Camp Meeting of the Church of God. I preached a very similar message on Wednesday evening to the one I had just preached on healing in Canada, yet as far as I know, no one was healed. God is sovereign. There is an unknown factor in healing. He simply knows more than we do!

One of the joys of our time in Dallas and the years that followed was that God gave me an evangelistic ministry around the USA and the world. Having had the privilege to preach in 40 states and in at least 12 countries, I've seen God show up and bless His people. Jesus is the same yesterday, today and forever. God will use those who seek him in many exciting ways. Even though we don't know how God does His miracles, we can be a part of what He is doing. He uses both the bad and the good to build us into ambassadors for Christ who can have an impact in the world. Our stories of God's supernatural work can help change many lives. When Jesus shows up we can expect Him to be Healer, Savior, Deliverer and Comforter. I give Him all the praise!

"The weapons we fight with are not the weapons of the World."
II Corinthians 10:4

Chapter 10
The Korean Story

In 1983, Judy and I were invited to Mokpo, South Korea to preach a week long city-wide crusade. This was a last-minute call because the speaker who was scheduled to preach had to cancel. We only had a week to prepare for our trip. While discussing the trip with the Church of God missionary serving in S. Korea, I learned that my translator would need a detailed word-for-word manuscript for every message. I was an outline preacher, not a manuscript preacher, and I was leaving town right before our trip for a mission's conference in Phoenix, Arizona. Out of a sense of desperation, I gave Alberta, my secretary, tapes of seven messages I had previously preached. I asked her to type them verbatim from the tapes. She typed all day and all night and then delivered them to Judy at 6:00 AM, literally hot off the press. Judy then left for the airport to join me on our flight to South Korea. I met Judy at the curb and exchanged my Phoenix suitcase for the one packed for South Korea. Judy parked the car and we barely made the flight that would eventually get us to South Korea. As I relaxed in my seat and began to look at the manuscripts that had been so hastily prepared, ink began to smudge and come off every place

I touched them. The term "hot off the press" was very descriptive of our situation. The ink had not dried on the paper. My long flight would involve the arduous task of tracing over all the typing with an ink pen so it would be usable. It took the entire flight to South Korea to prepare four of the seven messages.

When we finally arrived in Seoul, we were met by our translator, Pastor Chin, and a driver for the long six-hour trip to Mokpo. Mokpo is located on the southern tip of South Korea and has a population of 250,000. It is a highly Buddhist area with a mixture of Chinese and Japanese religions. The church that Pastor Chin led had about 600 adults and many, many children. It was a healthy, growing church, and was excavating for a new building to hold the 5000 people they were expecting to reach. Our meeting would not be held in a stadium or large facility, but in the excavated area for the new church building. As we spent hours together in the car, it became obvious to me why my interpreter needed my manuscripts to study. I was not able to communicate with him effectively. Neither of us understood the other beyond very simple words. This gave me a growing sense of insecurity about the week.

As we entered Mokpo, we were given a tour of the city. At each intersection or building, I saw posters advertising the crusade. My picture, along with Pastor Chin's, was staring at us all over the city. I heard cars with speakers on them blaring out invitations to the crusade. The insecurity I was feeling became even more intense when Pastor Chin translated the message. A challenge was ringing out through the speakers, "Come to the meetings tonight to see the one true God in action. You will see His miracles and His power."

Needless to say, this was a great motivation to my prayer life!

Korean Revival

Later that evening, I was told we were going to a church meeting in which I was to speak. This was not on the schedule, and my seven manuscripts did not cover this contingency. I grabbed one of my previously-prepared sermons and gave it to Pastor Chin. I now knew I would come up one short at some point. The evening went well, and I sensed that God was going to do some powerful things during the week. I was amazed by the discipline of the children. At least 100 children were jammed into the front of the sanctuary on the floor. They were almost sitting on top of one another. I never heard any noise from this group nor did I see them move much throughout the entire two-hour service.

We were then taken to a hotel room with mats on the floor for our first night's sleep. Our hosts spoke no English and we spoke no Korean, so our communication was sign language at best. The refrigerator had been filled with fruit; their hospitality was incredible. In fact, the hospitality during this week was so loving that we had to be careful what we requested, or they would get it for us. We learned that bragging on a food dish would bring four or five more of the same dishes in a row. The floors were hard and even a tired traveler had trouble sleeping that first night. I wonder if the reason Koreans get up to pray at 4:00 AM is that they can't sleep beyond this on their hard floors!

The next morning I was picked up just before 4:00 AM to attend a morning prayer meeting. I was shocked to see 200 people in attendance. We prayed for an hour, with everyone praying out loud in one accord. People were crying all over the room as they wept for the lost people in the city. The insecurity was starting to leave because of the evidences of God's heart and power among my new friends. Their faith and zeal touched me very deeply. I was interested in how the logistics of this worked. I asked, "Who goes out to pick up the people for the 4:00 AM prayer meeting?" I was told, "Whoever the pastor tells to do it." The bus was on the road by 3:00 AM.

As the first gathering of the week long crusade approached, people started streaming into the excavated area prepared for the new church. The ground was very rough and there were no chairs. They sat on the dirt or on little pieces of cardboard they had brought with them. There were approximately 2,000 people in attendance the first night. The typical pattern was to assemble at least an hour before the actual starting time and sing praise to the Lord before the service. The official service would then start with another hour of acappella praise. It was here with these wonderful brothers and sisters that we learned that praise is a powerful weapon for spiritual warfare. They believed that as they praised the Lord, the sounds would travel across the city, rendering the demons powerless. With their fervent prayer and powerful praise, they trusted God to bring unsaved people to the meetings. That is exactly what happened! After the praise time, there would be a lengthy testimony followed by the preaching. It would be late at night when the meeting finished and there would be very long altar response times. The crowd had grown to 10,000 by the end of the week.

One evening, the pastor asked my wife, Judy, if she would like to share a testimony in the service. I convinced Pastor Chin that he should let Judy preach because she has a ministry of inner healing that God really uses. This would also take care of the one sermon I was missing. After she shared part of her story, literally hundreds of people came to the altar. Her inspiring testimony was for women with harsh fathers or husbands who have a hard time responding to a loving heavenly father. She spoke about being reparented by the love of God. She wanted them to know that God is a loving heavenly father and they can trust him even if they haven't experienced love from their earthly fathers. This message met a huge need for women brought up in the Korean culture where they are often treated harshly by the men in their life. The front of the excavated area was filled with people responding to the love of God with tears and heart-felt thanksgiving.

Experiencing this week of praise, prayer, preaching, healing and deliverance shook my world. Not only did thousands of people come to Christ in salvation, but we saw great miracles every night of the crusade. The very first night a blind person was healed along with a lame man. This went on all week. An anecdotal note is that the first evening that I stood to preach, people laughed when they saw me at 6'4" standing beside Pastor Chin who was perhaps 5' tall. The second night, to ensure no more laughs, Pastor Chin came out with a box to stand on as he interpreted. This was his perch the rest of the week.

The last night of the crusade was on Sunday evening, and the presence of God was very powerful this night. When the service was over, no one moved. God was in that place, and all of us knew it. At the end of the service, I was asked to go through the massive crowd to pray a blessing on the people. They believed that the laying on of hands and prayer brought them great blessings. This looked like an impossible task since people were literally sitting on top of one another. There were no seats, no aisles, and no rows. It looked like sardines in a can, packed tightly into this small space. How do I get my size 12 shoes through this crowd? The shoes came off and we plunged in.

As we moved slowly through the crowd, laying our hands on people, I saw manifestation after manifestation of deliverance and healing. I saw people being thrown around by demons and then wonderfully delivered. I saw a man who had skin cancer all over his body be instantaneously cleansed when we laid our hands on him. He had been a Buddhist leader for over 30 years, but he gave his heart to Christ and followed us around like a child, wanting to know more about the Jesus who had just healed him.

Our time in Mokpo allowed us to witness many healings and we saw several thousand people make a decision for Christ. There were hundreds who were delivered from demonic bondage. We grew to love people in this missionary church as they prayed for the city. Today the completed church stands where we had our meeting. When I asked Pastor Chin how he was going to build the new church building when most of his people were very poor. He said, "One block at a time." What a testimony to faith in the promises of God! Our great God moved mightily among the people who attended the crusade, but Judy and I may have been impacted more than anyone else in Mokpo. What we experienced still challenges us to this day. We were both blessed and challenged by the amazing visitation of God in these meetings. When Jesus shows up, no one stays untouched. Even entire cities will bow to him.

"Remember this: Whoever sows sparingly will also reap sparingly, and whoever sows generously will also reap generously." II Corinthians 9:6

Chapter 11
Ft. Lauderdale or Bust

There is more than one way to heal from a ministry trauma. As Judy and I finished our twelfth year at First Church of God in Dallas, we began to sense the need for a change of location that would allow both the church and us to heal from our protracted time of stress. Our last two years in Dallas were very peaceful and affirming, but God was showing me it was time to move forward. We had a seven-year honeymoon, three years of excruciating pain and conflict and finally two years of peace. In these last two years, I realized that the vision I had shared with the congregation was somehow lost in the conflict of the previous years. It was during this time that Wayne Putman, our Associate Pastor, began to have a vision for the church. During our sabbatical, we drove through Dallas and dropped in for worship one Sunday morning. Arriving late, we intentionally sat in the back row, so we would not be noticed. As I worshipped, God put on my heart that Wayne would be the next pastor of the church. This came to pass when we left.

The Call to Plant

During the end of my time in Dallas, I was working on a Doctor of Ministry degree at Fuller Theological Seminary. One of the courses was a course on church planting. I had talked to two of my Associate Pastors, Bob Boyd and Wayne Putnam, about helping them plant a church, and I looked forward to learning more about it. During this class, I noted in scripture that often the more experienced leaders would plant a church and then turn it over to someone younger to pastor the people. This realization was the beginning point of my call to plant a church. I was relatively sure Judy wouldn't want to do a church plant, but when I suggested this possibility to her I was shocked when she said, "This could be a great challenge for us and I could get excited about it." There went any excuse I may have had to delay our next assignment. I was past 50 years old, and some told me that was too old to plant a church. I did realize that to be successful, we would need a younger couple to plant the church with us. Judy and I really began to pray about this. Thus, began the lengthy process of looking for this other key couple.

One day, while I was reading scripture and praying on the back porch of our house in Duncanville, Texas, I saw a mental picture of Judy and me out on the limb of a tree and Satan sawing the limb off behind us. This picture warned me of the battle to come in planting a church. At the same time, I felt that if Satan was not worried about us planting a new church, why would he pursue us with a saw in hand? I sensed God was getting ready to do something great. Some have said that faith is not the absence of fear but stepping out in spite of fear. This describes the mindset we had as we sat on the back porch discussing the excitement and the measure of fear that such a drastic change would bring. At that very moment our doorbell rang and our good friend, Diane Higgenbotham, came to visit. She was a lady "on a mission" and believed that she had heard a word from the Lord for us. That word was that we would plant a church and the church would become a church with both poor and wealthy worshipping together. Diane had little information about our plans. This helped us see God's design for the next steps in our journey. There will be more about this at the end of this chapter.

These two events together confirmed that we were to plant a church. As we prayed about a location, we wanted to plant in a community that did not have a church on every corner like Dallas. We looked at Seattle, Washington and at Ft. Lauderdale, Florida. In both cities, only about 6% of the population attended any kind of church, including cults. Both of us had aging, widowed mothers living in South Florida so Ft. Lauderdale became our selected target. There was a vast new community being built on the edge of the Everglades called Weston—the bull's eye within the target. This area was being built as a bedroom community for businesses that service Central and South America. It was very ethnically mixed and an "escape" community for many from Miami, New York and New Jersey. It was advertised as a community without crime and violence. I remember the large sign as one drove into Weston that said, "The only gangs in Weston are Boy Scouts and Girl Scouts."

Funding Our Dream

We were at a time of life where there were significant financial challenges starting with two daughters in college. We put a fleece before the Lord that if we were to do this plant, we needed Him to give us a glimpse of how He would fund this new church. Shortly after our prayers about this need, I met with Rev. Dan Hardin in Florida. I mentioned to Dan what we wanted to do, and he told me that he might have a way to help. He called some other pastors who were trustees of a fund that had been set aside for church planting in South Florida. He asked what amount was needed. My response was, "Enough money to pay for two full-time staff couples for two years." Within a week, Dan called me, saying that he had $170,000 for a church plant and that they would invest in our project. What a mighty God we serve!

The next call was to Bill Jerrils, the Director of Church Planting for the Church of God in the State of Florida. It was important to have his blessing and the blessing of the Church of God in Florida. Assured that the State Office would support this effort, we started planning for our move. It is interesting to note the battle that emerged at the very beginning of this process. One of the persons, who was so unhappy with our leadership in Dallas, called Bill Jerrils and tried to convince him that they should not call me to Florida. As Bill asked him multiple questions and listened to the answers, he became more and more convinced that I was exactly the kind of person who could successfully plant a church in South Florida. What Satan meant for harm, God turned to good.

FT. LAUDERDALE OR BUST

Start Up Challenge

We put our Dallas house on the market and I left for South Florida in August, 1989. I lived with my mother in Homestead, Florida, and made my office the McDonald's near the main entrance in Weston, a commute of about an hour. This restaurant allowed me to see Ft. Lauderdale culture up close and personal. Listening to conversations and casually talking to customers gave me a good insight into the area. We had no core group for this new church nor did we have a major sponsoring church. We only had support from the General Assembly of the Church of God in Florida. Bill Jerrils became my supervisor, friend and encourager. He also became my fishing buddy, as he would take me out deep sea fishing to unwind. The support of those giving money for the plant was greatly appreciated. Our most significant support team was the almost 100 prayer partners who prayed diligently for our new church plant. Some of these prayer partners also provided funds for us. A group of widows and senior adults from First Church of God, Dallas, sent us the pocket change that had been collected in their weekly Bible study. These were poor widows and people of limited resources, people who truly were sending us all they had. Nothing motivated me more to be diligent than the gifts of these faithful friends.

The search for a couple to help us plant continued. The new church needed a young couple who could identify with youth and had gifts and skills to lead worship. After speaking with nearly 30 potential candidates, I felt that none of them were what we needed. Some had a hard time realizing that a church plant starts with nothing. When they asked what kind of instruments we had, we said none. When they wanted to know who our worship team was, the answer was the same—we didn't have one. When one person asked how many we had in our orchestra, it was clear they had no clue what was ahead.

While attending a Board Meeting for Warner Press in Anderson, Jeff Barnes, who worked in music sales at Warner Press, was asked by management to take me to the airport. As I shared with him the story of what we were doing in Ft. Lauderdale, he got extremely excited about this opportunity. Later he talked to his wife, Tamira, who was in her last year of college at Anderson University. Then he called me and asked if they could come to Ft. Lauderdale for a visit. We had very limited knowledge of Jeff and Tamira so we made arrangements for them to stay with us for a week. There was no room for error in this decision. We arranged their flights, shared the vision, showed them the area, and quickly fell in love with them. Jeff resigned his brand new job at Warner Press, and Tamira left college in the middle of her senior year. They sold their first home that they had just bought, and came to Ft. Lauderdale to have an incredibly fruitful and powerful ministry. Jeff and Tamira were both talented musicians and both had a heart for evangelism. God put together His team for the church plant.

What would we call our new church? We were all sharing ideas and names, but we couldn't find one that really had hit the mark. While driving along the Everglades, I saw a sign talking about the Everglades sawgrass. People instantly knew where you were located when you mentioned the sawgrass. God put Sawgrass Community Church in my heart; it was just the right name for the new church. This name would let people know that we were on the west side of Ft. Lauderdale, near the area where the Everglades were being reclaimed and the future city of Weston was being built.

In the beginning, there was a simple strategy: Start with a core group to help us start the new church. We preferred working with people with little church background because they would not be mired down in traditions. We planned to build relationships with unchurched people and form small groups. These groups would then become the core of the future church.

Our move to Florida was scheduled in August of 1989. The sale of our house, which we thought was sold, fell through at the last minute. So, I left solo for Florida to start the church. Judy arrived in October after our house sold. Jeff and Tamira Barnes could not be with us until three weeks before the new church opened in March of 1999. As I got to know people in Ft. Lauderdale and understood the culture more, I found out it was a very different world than Dallas. It was 30% Jewish, and as you can imagine, most of them were not excited about a Christian church in the neighborhood. I got calls from Jewish people demanding to be taken off our mailing list, after we had sent a mailing about the new church to an entire zip code. People in the area were very cynical about churches and about people in general. They were very careful about forming close relationships because they had not learned to trust people. We were cautioned to be aware of scams in the area. A lot of this was the Miami/New York/New Jersey mind set. Most people indicated they were not willing to come to any small group meeting. They would say many times, "When you get your church up and going, let us know and maybe we will visit." Although a few people began to come to Christ, small groups were almost impossible to start.

One of our attempts to connect with people clearly brought home the major distrust and disinterest in the area. Our strategy to get to know people in our subdivision was to invite them to our house for a come-and-go dessert, where we would explain that we were planting a new church. We were very interested in meeting families in our neighborhood. We had invited Bill Jerrills so he could stay abreast of what we were doing. Our dessert bar, which was fit for a king, seemed to have enough food for our entire neighborhood. The only three people all afternoon were Bill, Judy and me. Not one person from the 200 hand-delivered invitations chose to be with us that day. It is somewhat funny, if you can survive the disappointment. Later I found out that some wanted to come but had last minute problems that made it impossible. Some later visited because of that invitation.

Though nothing is impossible with God, we began to understand that we needed to launch a church quickly if we were going to start something in the Weston area. We met with a few Christians in the area who were referred to us. Johnny, Janice and Stacey Walker, Tim McIntosh and Cindy Maldanado were all willing to help us start the church. Tim would later meet his future wife, Stacey, on a paddleboat at our house. Laurie Hare and other volunteers from First Church of God in Ft. Lauderdale helped us make telemarketing calls and mass mailings to area residents. We needed these people desperately to help carry out our "Phones for You" project. We developed a mailing list by calling 9000 families. Out of this project, we found 1100 families who were interested in being on the mailing list of a new church. Jeff and Melissa Kaminsky, who lived near us on our lake, were very helpful in many ways. They were our neighbors, and Jeff was our computer guru. He was very excited about the new church and also helped financially in the early days of the church.

The hours I spent in McDonald's produced good information about the area. We also did some door-to-door surveys to get an understanding of the needs of the people. Our target was non-Christian and unchurched people. People in the Weston area thought that church, as they had known it, was boring, judgmental and didn't deal with real life issues. They were also suspicious that churches just wanted their money. Obviously, people who felt this way were not going to be very eager to attend any church. We had to learn more about these people to understand their needs. One of Robert Schuller's vision statements for the Crystal Cathedral church was "Find a need and fill it."

What we found in a second survey was that they needed help making families work, since many had blended families. They needed help building strong marriages, wanting the zing back in their relationships. They wanted to build good character in their children, and they knew they needed to improve their parenting skills. They wanted to make their children AIDS ,drug and alcohol proof. They wanted to learn to handle financial pressure better. Many were unable to manage stress from both financial and great time pressure. Both spouses were working, with little quality time together.

Understanding these needs helped make us ready to begin an advertising campaign for the new church. We had to make sure this church was not going to be boring and would deal with real life issues. It was not going to be judgmental and was not interested in their money. Instead, on the positive side, we listed their felt needs and suggested that these were the needs the new church would help meet. We knew they needed Jesus Christ, but most of them didn't know this yet.

Our salaries were paid from the fund in South Florida, but all start-up expenses fell on us: school rent, office equipment, sound equipment, materials for mass mailings, graphic design person, etc. Everything had to be done well because the people we were trying to reach were business people, many of whom owned their own businesses. We personally had about $10,000 on our credit card, which eventually came back to us as the church grew. The provision of all these needs is another thing that happens when Jesus shows up.

We designed a brochure and other ads and sent them to various groups. Our mailing list, developed through the "Phones for You" project, received four separate mailings and two phone calls. The entire area with multiple zip codes received two mass mailings. The last piece mailed was an invitation to our Launch Service on Palm Sunday, March 1990. I remember riding through Weston and praying for the brochures as they were being delivered. I also remember thinking that much of the wealth of Weston was not being used to advance the Kingdom of God. I promised God that if He would allow us to reach those people, we would be faithful to pass on these resources to the mission field.

In order to make this Launch Service happen, we recruited about 30 people to come in to help us with childcare, worship leadership and general greeting. My daughters and some of their friends who were home on their Spring Break, came to help us on our first Sunday. It did not hurt our effort to have many beautiful young women to grace the parking lot and greeting table! A few people from other churches also volunteered their services for that first Sunday. The school we targeted to be our launch site was not yet completed so we met at Flamingo Elementary School. All of us were on pins and needles to see if anyone would show up. Prior to the service, I was sitting in the front of the "cafetorium," praying for the service. I was afraid to look back as people gathered for this kick-off Sunday. We had worked so hard and so long that we needed a demonstration of God's favor. When I finally stood as worship started, I looked around and saw that many people were in attendance. (154) What started as fear now became exhilaration at what God had done and we felt that all of our hard work was worth the effort. That very first Sunday, I shared my testimony, and 19 people gave their hearts to Christ. The second Sunday, which was Easter, found 72 people in attendance, the lowest attendance that we would ever see. Nine people gave their lives to Christ that morning. The transformation of these lives was a thrilling story. We were off and running with many new converts who needed help to grow in Christ. This church would grow to an average attendance of over 200 in the six years we led it. Most of these people were new converts and brought an exciting dimension to our church.

Our first major activity, other than a church service, was a picnic. We chose a site close to our Sunday meeting location. The church had only met three times, and we weren't sure how many, if any, would come to the park. We were thrilled that 73 people came to the picnic and everyone had a great time. Some of the challenges of a new church were obvious at this picnic. We told people to bring their own beverages, and for almost everyone the beverage of choice was Budweiser. My wife, Judy, pointed this out to me, and I remember telling her, "Don't worry, I won't drink any!"

This would start us on a journey of many experiences that showed us that working with unchurched people was very different from working with a traditional church. A volleyball game had very spirited competition, and the players' language sounded like a group of drunken sailors. This confirmed that we reached our target group, the unchurched and unsaved. It was a joy to see many of them become committed followers of Jesus Christ in the next year. We had more fun than we had ever experienced at a church picnic. They were hungry for real relationships, and fun events helped meet this need.

Guidelines for our church's ministry began to develop. One of the first steps was to make sure 10% of all income went to missions, both domestic and foreign. After a period of time, our leadership was asked to consider paying for a church to be built in India, even though Sawgrass Community Church was still meeting in a school. About five years into our existence, we had a Building Campaign to begin acquiring funds for a piece of land or a building. People pledged $125,000 to be paid out in three years. Our plan was to put the first $5000 in a village church building in South India. We did it by faith, not knowing how we could do this. Not too long after this gift was sent to India, I received a call from Crossings Community Church, telling us of a gift given for our church. Someone who had visited Crossings only three times saw a note in their church bulletin requesting prayer for Sawgrass Community Church. After the service, this person asked the pastor if Sawgrass would be a good place to do some year-end giving. The pastor, Marty Grubbs, assured him this would be a very helpful gift for the new church. He and his wife gave the offering to Crossings and we received a call, telling us of the good news. Amazingly, this gift was for $30,000 and came immediately after we gave $5000 for the Indian church. Crossings Community Church supported our church on a monthly basis for several years, and for this we are eternally grateful. Our new leadership team would never forget the miracle God performed because our desire was that this church would to learn to be a generous church.

Our staff was a great team with Rev. Jeff and Tamira Barnes leading worship and youth ministry. Our worship was not normal for a new church plant. We wanted people to get into the presence of the Lord even if they felt somewhat uncomfortable in it. This became a distinguishing asset of our church that drew many people into the life of our church. Jeff also built a great youth group. It was fantastic the way God brought this racially diverse group together—one-third Hispanic, one-third African-American or Islander Black and one-third Anglo. A large number of youth came to Christ. It was quite funny to watch Jeff trying to find one genre of Christian music the whole group liked.

Tamira initially helped with children and was the mainstay of our worship experience with her gifted use of the piano. Our greatest outreach was a children's musical that purposely recruited about two-thirds of the participants out of the community. It became a big project, involving seven costume changes for the children. Many parents were also recruited. Nearly 280 people attended this musical even though the church was averaging only about 100 at this time. Her vision for children's musicals became a yearly event. They rehearsed all summer and presented musicals on Grandparent's Day in September. She also taught private piano lessons and brought many people to the new church as she connected with people in the area.

Judy, my wife, was Church Administrator and event planner. She also was overseer for pre-school children's ministries. She was by far the most involved person at Sawgrass and kept everything organized and staffed. She was responsible for developing all the various teams of people that enabled the ministry of the church to flourish. Because of the emphasis on helping people discover and use their spiritual gifts for the Kingdom, she is the main reason that about 80% of Sawgrass members were involved in ministry roles. Judy also willingly offered our home for the church office and our screened porch as the church Fellowship Hall.

Some Stories of Transformation

Carol Lookretis was one of the people who accepted the Lord in one of our first services. Her life began to change right before her husband's eyes. Rocky had some connection to a New York Mafia family, and his reason for attending our church was to mock what he thought might be a scam of some kind. He was very suspicious of what we were doing and who we were. However, as he continued attending, God opened Rocky's heart.

Several of us went to Rocky and Carol's home to encourage them in their new faith. In our discussion with them, they both opened up and told us about Rocky's Vietnam experience. We learned that he would often wake up with great fear and anxiety, reliving some of his battles. At times, he would get in the fetal position behind a chair on the living room floor to try to drown out the images. We laid hands on Rocky, anointed him with oil and prayed for him and his family. Jesus showed up in a miraculous way. Rocky told us that as we prayed, he saw some chains that were on his body fall off and a prison door that held him was opened. God touched him, the nightmares subsided in his life, and he entered into a new dimension of freedom. Rocky has made it to Heaven before us, but his legacy lives on in Carol and in Carol's son, Chris, who Rocky helped raise. Chris is now a lead Pastor, and his testimony has led many to Christ. He was a product of Jeff's youth ministry and was called by the Lord to His service.

Another transformation story is that of Greg Stamatis. Greg and his wife, Holly, lived on the same lake as we did in Davie, Florida. Later I learned that Holly had received one of our new church mailings and had put it on the refrigerator as a church she hoped to visit. One day Holly and I met as we were both walking around the lake. When she heard that I was a pastor, she was quick to point out that she was a believer. She told me that her husband, Greg, had recently accepted the Lord through a Christian radio program. She had prayed for him for many years. He had heard the gospel while driving and had pulled his car off the road and accepted Christ. Greg tried to find a church that would simply teach him the basics of the Christian life, but he could not find one that met his need. After accepting Holly's invitation, I went to Greg's house to meet him. He had a hungry heart for God. I told him about a Discovery Class for new Christians that I was beginning and challenged him to be part of it. I also laid out a vision for him to possibly teach this class at some future time. Within a few months, Greg was teaching the new Christian class and helping many new believers grow. He also began to train others to teach the class.

As I met with Greg weekly and watched him devour my seminary books, I learned he was an insatiable reader. For five years we meet each week and built one another up in the Lord. Greg and Holly became part of our Leadership Team at Sawgrass, and Greg went on to plant and pastor a church. He was and is an intelligent and powerful man of God whom God uses greatly.

Greg learned much about ministry and reached out to a lot of people. One night he had an unexpected and unusual encounter. I was driving a van and he was in the back seat with a man he was trying to help get free in Christ. As Greg began to put his hands on and pray for this man, a legion of demons manifested themselves. The man jumped all over the back of the van, causing the van to swerve back and forth on the road. When I looked at Greg, he looked like he had seen a ghost. After this encounter, he was very teachable as to how to do deliverance.

Phil and Julia Keeler came into our church several weeks after we opened. My first image of Phil is etched in my mind forever. He arrived in shorts, which is common in Florida, had a large wooden cross around his neck and a large family Bible under his arm. He came on a morning when we were asking a group of our new converts to stand in the front of the church and give public testimony that Christ was in their lives. When this group came forward at the end of the service, Phil and Julia were standing among them. I had not met them at that point, but when I visited them the next week, I learned that they came from a Catholic background. They had just made a commitment to Christ in our church that Sunday. Phil owned a large meat delivery business with many employees. One of his employees, Ray Kuhn, had invited him to our church. Phil also had been a professional drummer and quickly began playing in our worship band.

When this couple came to Christ, they really surrendered. Phil and Julia went through the New Christian Class taught by Greg. He began to lead some of his employees to the Lord, and several of them began to attend our church. He became involved in small group leadership and helped some of our new Christians grow. Although I haven't been able to confirm this, I have heard that Phil was teaching people how to overcome the strategies of the enemy in spiritual warfare. What a privilege to walk with such disciples of Christ!

One final story of a transformed life needs to be shared. Bill* had gone to a very liberal East coast school and had a world view very different from Christianity. Lorna,* his wife, was Jewish, so she was somewhat uncomfortable with the church and the message. They came for a while, mostly because their children really loved the church and put pressure on their parents to come. We discovered that on many Sunday mornings, Bill and Lorna often left church very angry over something I would say that did not fit their world view. Bill would also remark that it made no sense to him that I had left an engineering career to become a pastor. He knew the compensation for a pastor was much lower than for an engineer.

After about six months, they stopped coming and my attempts to call them were futile; he refused to return my calls. After hearing nothing from him for almost a year, he finally called. It was unforgettable. Bill confessed that when they were in the church their family life and marriage had improved. He told me he finally understood what I had shared about Christ being the center of my life. He asked almost apologetically if I could meet with him. He said, "I don't know why you should meet with me since I didn't even return your calls after we left the church."

For my part, I was very excited to meet with Bill and learn what God had done. He told me how life had not worked very well since they left the church, and he remembered the messages about what Christ could do in someone's life. He didn't know if he had done it right, but he had asked Jesus to be the center of his life, and now everything was changing. He mentioned that Lorna had not yet come to the same point, but if they were allowed, they would like to come back to the church. I rejoiced with him in his new life in Christ.

Bill and Lorna returned to the church, and Lorna soon joined her husband in following Christ. Bill and Lorna then developed a powerful ministry to couples who worked for Bill at Disney. They invited people who worked at Disney to their home in order to tell them what God had done for their marriage. Bill then got involved with a Cowboy Church since he was a horseman. He began to share his testimony in this new environment, too. They had a guest house on their property and they moved a jobless, single mom and her children in to live there. He then helped her to get a job at Disney. They were sharing what Christ had done for them with others. The last time I was at Sawgrass Community Church, Lorna was an integral part of the worship team and in charge of the drama team. When Jesus shows up, everything is different.

It is very important for us to remember that there is a war that goes on for every new believer. My understanding is that several years after we had left Sawgrass, this marriage failed. Bill moved to Los Angeles for a new job which took him away from his family and his church in Florida. Lengthy times apart allowed Satan to steal what the Lord had given them, which is what Satan loves to do. Pray for this couple. God loves them and knows their need.

An overview of what God did at Sawgrass was to bring a very diverse body of believers together from nine different nationalities. We were a mixture of ethnic groups, people who had Catholic backgrounds but hadn't attended church for 10, 20 and/or 30 years, people who were Jehovah Witnesses and people who were Mormons. As I previously stated, over 200 people accepted Christ into their lives in the first five years, and over 160 were baptized—in the ocean, in nearby lakes and in pools. The church continues to this day as a witness in South Florida to the transformation Christ can bring.

I want to thank all the wonderful leaders and lay people of Sawgrass Community Church: Johnny and Janice Walker, Tim and Stacey McIntosh, Morris and Glennie Simmons, Phil and Julie Keeler, Frank and Thelma Hardy (Frank is in Heaven waiting for us), Warren and Holly Tyree, Tim and Chris Prater, Bob and Jacquelyn Stewart, George and Cindy Joseph, Mick and Brenda Lasher, Pat Hardee, Elaine Simmons, Connie Bennett, Jeff and Vicky Botsford, George and Deloris Cambell, Brent and Ashleigh Sharp, Fraser and Barbara Casey, Mack and Susan Moore, John and Danielle Giglione, Lee and Darlene Kurtz, Greg and Holly Stamatis, Roger Trca, Alan Scherer, Art Gauer, Janet Jefferson and Joe Rich, plus all those people previously mentioned in this chapter and any others I forgot. (God knows!)

I have also told about the huge investment that Jeff and Tamira Barnes made. They were as much the planters as we were, and were wonderful witnesses and disciplers. I will always be awed by their commitment and effectiveness in our church plant. They are still a wonderful team for the Lord to this day! This gives you a picture of the beautiful body of Christ at Sawgrass Church.

I also give great credit to the pastors that followed me at Sawgrass. Lowell Hunking was an attorney from Canada. He was so gifted at making a case for Christ, excellent at apologetics. Some remarked that we were a great one-two punch because I taught them to worship from the heart and Lowell taught them to worship from the mind. He pastored less than two years and went home to Canada due to the illness of his daughter.

Rev. Terry Bernard was the next Pastor. He and his wife, Jill, spent a large part of their life with Sawgrass Community Church. They excelled in Children's ministries and felt right at home in the South Florida culture. Terry had come to the church from the business world. A pastor for 17 years plus, he had a great evangelistic and discipleship heart.

Rev. Christine Doty is the current pastor of Sawgrass (2018), a passionate leader with a great hunger for God. She has great challenges as the church still does not have a building to call its own after all these years. Sawgrass continues to win and send people. I take my hat off to those who have followed and hope as you read, you will pray for the church.

As previously stated, we didn't really want to start our church with many people with church backgrounds because many churches are not effective at winning people to Christ. We wanted Sawgrass Community Church to really focus on unchurched and unsaved people. In about the third year of the church, it became obvious that we desperately needed more mature Christians to help disciple all the new Christians. With so many young believers, we began praying for God to start sending more mature believers, which He did. The list above contains many of them. We were grateful for God's provision.

One of the side stories was that Hurricane Andrew came through South Florida in 1992 and destroyed the homes of my mother, my mother-in-law and my sister, Joyce. All of them lived with us for a time, and my sister and her husband, Tom, my mother and my mother-in law all relocated in Ft. Lauderdale. This was a wonderful season when many of our family members were together in Sawgrass Community Church. This was a great growth time for my niece, Tracey, and for all of our family. My sister, Joyce, was a very committed believer who really became centered in Christ after Judy and I were converted. She has since gone on to be with the Lord. I had the privilege to share her testimony at her funeral, using her Bible and her prayer lists. Her testimony, as shared by many at her memorial service, impacted people from all over the world. She was a bright light for Christ and I look forward to seeing her "in the morning."

The Original Prophecy

God brought both the rich and the working class poor to Sawgrass just as Diane Higgenbotham's prophecy had said. When planning for the church plant, we targeted the Weston area on the west side of Ft. Lauderdale. This community only had 1500 homes in 1989, but it was developed for 60,000. When we arrived, the development was so new there was no place for a church to meet in Weston. There were no schools in those early days, nor were there other venues for worship. We had to move into a school about two miles from our target area, on the edge of a mobile home park that had lower-middle class and some very poor people. The community had a very high crime rate and a reputation for drug usage. As we began to worship in this school, we started reaching many in the mobile park who were struggling to make ends meet.

About a year later, a school opened in Weston. We had been on a waiting list to rent the Indian Trace

Cafetorium for worship and a few small rooms for children. The problem was that Weston was high-middle class to extremely wealthy. The typical home in Weston was over $250,000 up to Dan Marino's multi-million dollar home. We were concerned about how well our more modest class of people would handle moving with the church into such an upscale community. We were greatly relieved when we found out that our relationships were deep enough that people made the move with us. We immediately began to also attract people from Weston. We ended up with CEO's of companies and many executives and owners of businesses in the area. We had a wonderful balance of the poor and rich, and through Christ they became one body. We were Hispanic, Anglo, African-American, Islanders, rich and poor. What a beautiful picture of Heaven!

How could this small church in a very resistant area see so many people come to Christ? I believe it was because 100 prayer intercessors punched a hole between Weston and Heaven, and that God answered the part of the Lord's prayer that says, "Thy Kingdom come, your will be done on earth as it is in Heaven." We also had a culture of prayer and fasting at Sawgrass that will be mentioned in Chapter 13. Thank you, Jesus, for showing up at Sawgrass Community Church and bringing so many people to Yourself!

"How great is the love the Father has lavished on us, that we should be called children of God!" I John 3:1

Chapter 12
The Girls at Hope Hill

One of the joys of retirement is to awake in the morning and never know what unexpected challenges might lie ahead. That was certainly true in the case of a call I received in 2012 to be the Interim Pastor at First Church of God in Mt. Sterling, Kentucky, east of Lexington. God had sent us in many different directions through the years, frequently putting us in situations which we did not know how to handle. God was always faithful in those times. He led us and directed us as we listened to Him.

This church was dealing with the unexpected resignation of their much-loved Senior Pastor. We were asked to come prepared to stay for one year, so that they could search for a new Senior Pastor. The need for stability and guidance through a time of pastoral transition is critical, not only for the staff and leaders of the church, but also for those in the congregation. The existing church leadership needed affirmation and support. Sunday messages needed to be practical and gospel centered. One thing I am certain of is Jesus' promise in John 12:32 when He said, "But I, when I am lifted up from the earth, will draw all men unto myself." Through Jesus, God could and would bring real surprises and times when the miraculous invaded our midst. Such was the case for the time that we lived and ministered at Hope Hill.

We volunteered to live in our RV while doing the interim in Mt. Sterling. When we arrived, we were instructed to park at what was formerly known as Hope Hill Children's Home. Due to changes in our culture, an orphanage was no longer needed within the Church of God community. Hope Hill had transitioned into a residential alternative school for girls, approved to house about 45 teenage girls. The girls living there were assigned by the court for a mandatory period of time. They would live and attend school at Hope Hill. Anything that would take them away from the property would have to be highly supervised.

Hope Hill is located in a beautiful country setting. The tranquility of the rolling hills and the beauty of the farms around Lexington was very refreshing. We camped on the back of the property, while the girls were housed toward the front. At first, we had no interaction with the girls, but they would see us driving in and out. I'm sure they were curious about these strangers who were in their midst.

Hope Hill had always been a Christ-centered ministry. However, these girls were placed there by the courts due to major conflicts with their public schools and families. Education had definitely not been a priority in their lives. Some girls had been in foster care and bounced from place to place most of their lives. Others had been the victims of parental neglect, of sexual abuse, of drug and/or alcohol addiction, etc. I remember that one girl, whose mother was mentally ill, shared how she had to be the parent to her mother.

Truthfully, we had little in common with these girls. Slowly we began to have more contact with them, but they didn't show any real interest in us or the church. I began to be aware that a few of the girls were attending the Sunday services at the church. Judy and I started to encourage and show the love of Christ to these girls. After about three months at the church, God really began to draw the hearts of some of the girls to Christ and a few were wonderfully saved. While we were excited about their interest and decisions, we knew that follow-up to their conversion was critical. Reverend Paul Sanders was overseeing the chapel services and spiritual activities for the girls, so we met with him to discuss how to encourage these new believers and help them grow in faith. We discussed the need for a Bible class for both the new believers at the church and for the Hope Hill girls who had recently accepted Christ. There were many restrictions regarding where the girls could go and what they could do, and it became apparent that they needed their own separate Bible class.

After our discussion, Paul asked if we'd come to one of their weekly chapel services and speak to the girls. These services were not mandatory, and we were told that they never knew how many girls would participate. Paul introduced Judy and me as the chapel speakers for the day I was to speak, but as I looked at these teenagers, I felt a strong leading that Judy needed to share her story with them. She could speak from her heart about an alcoholic father and a dysfunctional family life that had left many emotional scars in her life. First, I spoke to the girls about a few young women mentioned in Scripture whom God had used mightily.

I wanted them to see that they were not too young to have an important Kingdom impact. Then Judy spoke about the healing and restoration that was available to those who were hurting emotionally.

These girls had previously been given no forum with which to share their own stories with each other. Many stories were so horrid that they could potentially cause great depression and anger in the girls. Telling our own stories really opened the girls to the work of the Holy Spirit. God was working deeply in their hearts, rooting out issues that had caused such great pain in their lives. We challenged the girls to be part of a new Bible class that we would offer in their dining hall. Anyone could attend, but we especially wanted all the new believers to be present. Again, Hope Hill couldn't require that anyone attend. We weren't sure they would want to listen to two people in their late 60's and mid 70's. We simply prayed for God to use us and asked for favor among the girls.

It was very exciting to see about 15 girls come for our first session. Some of these girls had attended the church services in Mt. Sterling, but some had not. Since we were dealing with all young girls, Judy was the main teacher. I would pray, introduce my wife, and help serve the snacks. A few times I shared in the teaching, but Judy's gift of communication and the story of her path to victory were what the girls really needed. We quickly learned that it's not only guys who become pliable when there is food, but also these girls. We treated them with a good snack at every meeting. It took a while for us to gain a place of trust with the girls, so we just loved on them and tried to help them understand how special they were. We also spent a lot of time simply listening to them. The class started out with some simple materials listing five assurances that a believer has: salvation, answered prayer, guidance, forgiveness, and victory over the lies, deception and strongholds of the enemy.

Due to her own personal struggle in this area, Judy felt there was little hope for victory if the girls didn't gain great assurance of their identity in Christ. That led to several weeks trying to deeply embed these truths in these young lives. It became more and more apparent that these girls wore ugly scars, given to them primarily by people who should have loved them. Some of their scars were also self-inflicted wounds. Their "trusters" had been broken or deeply damaged. How could they really trust anyone, let alone a God they couldn't see? Could they really believe that God loved them? Did He really love each girl so much that He would pay the penalty for her sins by dying on the cross? Would He really forgive them for all the terrible things they had done? Instead of condemnation, would He really give them abundant, Eternal Life? Did He really have a wonderful plan for their lives?

We watched in amazement as the group grew from 15 to 20 to 25. The girls living at Hope Hill were taking part voluntarily, and the weekly snacks proved to be a good motivation. A cookout at the end of the class also motivated them to participate regularly. Anyone who completed the work and attended 75% of the classes was invited to participate. All of them qualified!

More and more, they wanted to talk about life and their future. They had hundreds of questions. Some of these girls who had been arrested and charged with all kinds of anti-social behaviors gave rapt attention to

Judy as she taught. One by one they started giving their hearts to the Lord. Miraculous moves of God were transpiring right before our eyes in the lives of girls that the typical church wouldn't want in their midst. After all, they probably reasoned, these girls might be a bad influence on the church kids. They would have been perceived as being too hardened, beyond reaching. In truth, we found these girls broken, desperately needing someone to love and accept them. They wanted someone to help them find hope.

We planned a special experience to try to help the girls know that they could be forgiven regardless of what they had previously done. We wanted them to have assurance that all their sin was forgiven by Christ if they would simply trust Him, so we decided to have a lesson on forgiveness. At the end of the class we gave each girl a sheet of paper and asked them to list all the sins that they could remember committing. This list was for their eyes only. A cross was in the middle of their page. We had been told earlier not to give any homework assignments to these girls because they wouldn't do them. We decided to take a chance and ask them to do it anyway, all the while wondering if they would bring the lists back to class. We gave them scriptural guidance for the project. When class time came around the next week, we found girls coming in so excited, waving their "personal sin list" and exclaiming to one another how many sins they listed. It seemed as their boasting was in how bad they had been. One girl proudly announced that she had 54 sins on her list!

After teaching on forgiveness that night, we shared the pain and humiliation that Jesus had suffered for them. We prayed urgently that God would help them understand that He loved them so much that He went through the horror of Calvary so they could be forgiven. We then went outside for a very visual experience. Christ had indeed paid the penalty for their sin and He was calling them to a new life. We emphasized that the next part of what we were going to do should definitely not be done if they truly didn't mean it. We started a fire and the girls encircled it. One by one, they each took their list to the fire pit, ignited it and watched their sins go up in smoke. However, one girl did not burn her sin list. The others were all filled with joy and excitement to think that after all these years God held nothing against them and was calling them to a new life filled with hope and love. Afterwards, the girl who didn't participate came to me and said that before she could burn her list, she felt that she needed to be saved. What a great privilege to introduce her to Christ and pray with her. She glowed like a beautiful lamp after inviting Jesus into her life and she was thrilled to take her list to the fire and burn it. We will never forget that wonderful evening's experience when Jesus showed up.

One of the counselors at Hope Hill had been saved at the church a few weeks earlier. She, like the girls, was a new Christian and was taking part in the new Christian class at the church. One of the girls, who had started coming to the Bible study at Hope Hill, approached her with an observation and a question. She asked the counselor if she had been saved because she had been watching her look up Scripture for her Bible study. But it wasn't just working on the assignment that got her attention; it was a noticeable change in her behavior.

Apparently, the counselor's vocabulary had been quite bad, filled with much swearing and temper. But all of a sudden that changed, and when she slipped up, she asked the girls to forgive her. When the girl found out that her counselor had truly been saved, she was very excited and stated that if that counselor could be saved then she could be saved, too. She thought she had been way too bad to be forgiven and that there was no hope for her.

We don't really know how many of these young girls accepted Christ while we were at Hope Hill; we think perhaps around 20-25. Some were quite vocal about their new life. Those who have been forgiven much, love much. (Luke 7:47) Even after we left Hope Hill, the Bible study continued to help them solidify their decisions and to learn how to walk out their new life in Christ.

As promised, the picnic became a celebration of the girls' new lives. We played games together and enjoyed some great barbeque. We loved on these girls and felt their love in return. After dinner, we asked the girls what they had experienced in the past few weeks at the class. Several of them began to tell their own personal stories, which tore our hearts. One girl shared that her grandfather, father and brother had all raped her. She medicated herself with drugs. Many had become alcohol and drug dependent just trying to diminish the pain they regularly felt in their hearts. But one new theme had invaded these stories. It was the seed of hope that Jesus Christ brings.

Scripture tells us that no matter how deep the suffering we experience, God will use us to touch others. (II Corinthians 1:5) Judy's initial feeling about being involved with these girls was that she was being thrown into the middle of a situation where she had a hard time finding common ground with these girls. Through the years she had been accused by some of her friends as being "Goody Two Shoes." However, God showed her that she, like all those girls, had come to a fork in the road. She had taken the path of least resistance, desiring to stay out of conflict, to not "rock the boat." These girls took another path. They were not willing to sit quietly by, allowing others to abuse them. They were not about to be ignored, but would strike out, causing problems for those who hurt them. They were responding to their world with hate and anger. God does not want us to take either of those two paths. He wants us to experience His love and forgiveness, leading us to walk joyfully into a healthy freedom. He wants to walk the road with us, reparenting us as we go. When Jesus shows up, our entire lives can change, and we can begin to live the life He designed us to live. We find the destiny for which he created us. We believe a wonderful group of young girls did just that!

"Don't you know that you yourselves are God's temple and that God's Spirit lives in you? If anyone destroys God's temple, God will destroy him; for God's temple is sacred, and you are that temple." I Corinthians 3:16-17

Chapter 13
The Kendall Intervention

The intent of this book is to show what happens when Jesus shows up in our everyday lives. In discussing the Kendall miracle, I will purposely refrain from using actual names of those involved.

Judy and I were enjoying our retirement in Texas when a call came from the State Office of the Church of God in Florida. I was asked if I could do an interim pastorate for what I assumed would be a few months at Kendall Community Church of God in Miami, Florida. This was somewhat challenging since I was 76 and had been having some health issues. Recently I had also passed out multiple times due to heart and blood pressure problems.

I learned quickly from candid discussion with Florida leaders that this was a very troubled church. Some local church members had filed a lawsuit against the Board of Directors of the church, the General Assembly of Florida and the previous Senior Pastor. This had become a very incendiary incident which had badly polarized the church. The leadership of the Church of God in Florida had a team of outstanding leaders trying to help the church, but the plan to help was rejected.

The people of Kendall did not trust outsiders who were trying to help their church. The on-going turmoil led to growing distrust and alienation inside the church. Some of the Florida leaders voiced concern for their personal safety when coming to the church because of all the animosity. One of these leaders warned me that this was the only church he had ever visited where he felt he needed to carry a gun for self-defense. He said this with tongue in cheek, but on a previous visit someone had tried to run him down with a car in the church parking lot. We had a lot of warnings that relationships had deteriorated badly at Kendall, but when we finally arrived it was even worse than we expected.

A logical question is why did we go to Kendall? We had a wonderful built-in excuse because of my age and health issues. Isn't this the time to slow down rather than enlist in a full-time, stress-filled job? The only answer is that when Judy and I prayed about this interim offer, God began to give us a burden for the people. Because we had some prior history with this church, we decided to go. I remember leading conferences and preaching on a Sunday morning to over 650 people when I was State Coordinator of the General Assembly of the Church of God in Florida. Also, Kendall Church was a major donor with other South Florida churches that helped us plant Sawgrass Community Church in Ft. Lauderdale in 1989. In some sense, I felt that I owed the church for making it possible for us to plant a church. I needed to try to help them. I was also excited about the thought of being Interim Pastor for a multicultural church. This church consisted predominately of Jamaicans and Islanders. The staff was composed of people from Puerto Rico, Ghana, Guyana, Cuba, the Bahamas and now us from Texas. All of my life, I have had a great interest in the unity that God can bring in diversity, so I was eager to be part of a community like Kendall. In a period of two weeks, we heard about the possibility, decided to go, packed our car and began the journey. There was hardly room for us in our SUV; every nook and cranny was filled. Our next adventure had begun, and what we thought would be three months turned into 20 months.

It is very difficult to set the stage for all that had happened and was happening at Kendall Church. This church had a history of being a church of nearly 600 plus people from 69 nations. In the 70's, 80's, and 90's, it became one of the most well known churches in the community. However, over a period of time there were some leadership failures that hurt the church. The current lawsuit had been spawned by the latest of these transgressions. It alleged that the Senior Pastor had misdirected funds from church accounts to his own personal account. This had badly divided the church between those who supported the pastor and those who didn't. When troubles began to accelerate, the church went into serious decline—from a congregation of about 350 to one of 100 or less. A young adult ministry that had been flourishing withdrew from the church and became a ministry of its own because the leaders wanted to protect the young adults from all the strife and division in the church.

Initially, the former pastor was accused of misdirecting about $3,500 from church accounts into his own account. He was confronted with this, admitted the indiscretion, and paid this money back to the church. He expressed sorrow that it had happened and assured both the local church leaders and the state leaders of the General Assembly of the Church of God in Florida that this was the extent of the problem. He was to step down for a period of time and go through counseling. Stirring the waters further, while temporarily removed from his leadership position, the pastor called for a vote of confidence and won majority support, even though there was a feeling among some that the outcome was questionable. Even with this vote going against them, many who filed the lawsuit still believed the transgression was much more than the $3,500 that had been discovered earlier.

Much more time elapsed before it was known that $3,500 was just the tip of the iceberg. The court became embroiled in the process, and the legal battle continued to rage. The pastor was finally removed from the church and the family was ordered out of the parsonage. It was later discovered that over $75,000 was misappropriated. Attorneys subpoenaed the pastor's Illinois bank records and were able to then prove the $75,000 misappropriation. At the end of this process, the pastor was found guilty of grand theft and was ordered by the court to reimburse the church $500 per month until the church was repaid.

As with most pastoral failures, some people opted for a process of reconciliation with the pastor while others felt very strongly that the pastor should be fired. Further complicating this particular situation was the fact that this was the first black pastor the church had ever called, and all were hoping he would succeed. He was a very charismatic figure and had a powerful pulpit presence. Some in the congregation were people he led to the Lord. He had been in various leadership positions, even at the national level of the Church of God.

Some leaders felt that the only way to resolve the issues was to file a lawsuit. Some of those who wanted the pastor to leave had been some of his closest friends. They were deeply hurt by their pastor's betrayal. They felt that the Board of Directors of the church was protecting the pastor and pushing back against anyone involved with or sympathetic to the lawsuit. This group felt that their appeals to the Board of Directors were ignored. On the other side, the Board of Directors felt the lawsuit was not initiated in a biblical way. They responded by attempting to discipline the people who filed and financed the lawsuit. A vote of the congregation took place to remove all members who were attached to the lawsuit in one fell swoop. They were all listed on a ballot where a single vote removed the entire group. Those who filed the lawsuit were thus all removed from membership. Later, the court stated that this was an illegal action. The vote needed to be for each person individually, giving each an opportunity for rebuttal. After the judge's admonition, the church did not pursue removing any person from membership.

Relationships eroded to the point that there was little trust in the body. Long-time friends and even family members were divided over the lawsuit. The Board of Directors did not trust the 30 or so people who started, supported and/or financed the lawsuit. The group who sued did not trust the Directors to deal with the pastor. Both groups of people were certain that Satan was leading the other side, and every attempt to resolve the issues failed. Each time there was a business meeting, all this anger and hurt poured out from people on both sides. Business meetings became shouting matches. My first business meeting seemed like urban warfare. One long-term church member used the Lord's name in vain very loudly and defiantly. It was not unusual at this time for people in the church to interrupt services in order to make accusations. Welcome to the "Kendall wars." In the past, people had been so unruly in business meetings that the police were called to keep order. The police had posted signs on the property that they had the right to remove anyone from the property who was out of order. One of these signs was placed right in front of the main entrance to the church. What a terrible message for visitors to see! I removed it and hid it in my office, but later I learned that this was illegal, so I had to put it back up. How do you find a way to bring reconciliation in a situation like this? This would be a constant prayer of my heart!

An example of the state of the church became obvious my first day at Kendall. I quickly received a briefing on which people I could and could not trust. I was also advised that I couldn't trust all the staff. I felt like I had entered an undercover FBI investigation. When we first arrived at the church, there was a funeral in progress. It was pointed out to me that some of the people at the funeral were not the good guys but rather the bad guys. I was told this group wouldn't want to talk to me. This motivated me to shake every hand in each group of people, making solid eye contact with every person. I was reminded once again that we are all made in the image of God, and this gives every one of us inherent value. This was the beginning of a new day at Kendall.

The church decided to support the Board of Directors so they agreed to pay all the expenses of the lawsuit. These expenses ultimately totaled over $200,000. Those who started the lawsuit also spent nearly $200,000 out of their own pockets. The result was a major drain of resources from the church that could have destroyed it if the lawsuit continued. Some of this money was later replaced by insurance money, but even this required more lawyer expense. The only people who benefited from the lawsuit were the two lawyers.

Accusations, alienation, charges, counter charges, anger, hurt, bitterness, lack of forgiveness and public out cries were our weekly experiences. There were times when I would ask Judy, "Tell me again. Why we are here?" Truth was elusive. Both groups saw their own viewpoint as truth. My problem was that I was about the only one talking to both groups. As they talked, I saw some justification in the view of each group and some distortion in the views of each group. Both accused people on the other side of being criminals and monsters. The anger that each side felt was believed to be righteous indignation. My view was that Satan was working on each side to do what he always does—kill, steal and destroy. John 10:10 NIV

On my fist Sunday at the church, I made it clear that I would not be on either side in the battle. I told them I would be on Jesus' side. This meant several things to me:

1. Everyone has value and inherent worth because they are made in God's image and because Jesus died for them.
2. Only Jesus, the Prince of Peace, could pull this church back together.
3. Our intercessors were the key to releasing the Kingdom of God in our midst. I believed that the Kendall intercessors were the only hope for bringing the church together. Judy and I both believed that this group of people prayed us to Kendall! God heard their cries and prompted our hearts to be drawn there.
4. We needed to follow God's vision to the cross. One night I had a dream, in which people were moving towards the cross. Some were far away and some close. The closer we got to the cross the more we would see people like Jesus saw them. Getting close would cause us to say with Jesus, "Father, forgive them, they know not what they do." This forgiveness needed to be offered to the offending pastor who misappropriated the money, and to everyone else, even those considered enemies.
5. I had no ability in and of myself to bring any measure of reconciliation to Kendall. If God did not do it, it would not be done.
6. If, after my tenure at Kendall, everyone thought I was a great preacher, I would have failed. However, if that same group of people would see a more powerful and more available Jesus by the end of our assignment, I would have succeeded.

The lawsuit became the symbol of all that divided us. It became a testimony for the way the enemy can bring destruction to the Body of Christ. It was a haunting reminder that we were not free to be what God wanted us to be. The lawsuit would have to go, but how? All of us prayed diligently for a breakthrough. I had never felt so dependent on God because human answers were not going to suffice. As Interim Pastor, my major assignment was the healing of the congregation. The truth is that most of my time was involved in the lawsuit and all its negative effects on the church.

In the early days of ministry at Kendall, I felt that my priority was to preach through the book of I John. This book dealt with love, forgiveness and the folly of hatred. This same theme was picked by the young adult leader who had also felt directed by the Lord to take our Wednesday night Bible study through this same book. The Word of God is the power of God unto salvation. As this was read, shared, preached and prayed over, it began to touch hearts. Some change began to be observed. Secondly, I did all I could to embolden and encourage the intercessors. Tuesday night prayer meeting was my highest priority and my greatest joy. I knew the battle was the Lord's and we could only see His victory if we were on our knees. Tuesday's intercession powerfully influenced everything in the church. An example is that there was unrest and a lack of unity in the worship team. At a very critical time, God brought a spirit-filled worship leader to us who stayed about a year. She taught us about worship and was extremely sensitive to the leading of the Holy Spirit.

Thirdly, I tried to be a good listener to both sides of the conflict. Some healing came simply by expressing hurts and anger. The gulf was great, and forgiveness was not given easily. Meeting with people on both sides who were stuck in the mire of hatred and unforgiveness brought me great stress. I learned that if we allowed hatred to prevail long enough, it would capture us and we will become pawns to it. The writer of Hebrews states, "See to it that no one misses the grace of God and that no bitter root grows up to cause trouble and defile many." (Hebrews 12:15)

At times, while meeting with people in the middle of the conflict, I felt like I was talking directly to Satan. This broke my heart, as I had grown to love people on both sides of the gulf. Darkness, blindness, bitterness, confusion, judgments, etc. were constant companions in the process. I must be honest and say that at times the pressure was too great for me to bear. A few times I went to Judy and told her that if I didn't leave Kendall, I would die there. God knew what He was doing when he gave me my helpmate. Judy was so strong and sure of our call to Kendall that she would lovingly encourage me to keep fighting the good fight of faith. She was too busy to think of retreating because she had totally recreated a nursery and toddler's ministry for children. She had redecorated two rooms, recruited staff and trained staff for these important ministries. She was also working in the office and deeply involved in doing research on the lawsuit. The people of Kendall were moving deeper and deeper into both of our hearts, so we stayed the course.

The desperation for God's solution continued. If the lawsuit did not get settled, it was going to go to a public trial. This could have cost the church and the plaintiffs another $100,000 each. Even worse was the bad testimony it would bring. It also offered a threat to the different Directors who were personally sued. My most fervent prayer was for a way to kill the lawsuit, the symbol of our division.

One of the common complaints of the plaintiffs was that the church paid for the Directors expenses, but they had to pay for the lawsuit out of their own pockets. As I prayed about this, a small light began to shine. It is important to note that if I would have tried to get the church to give the plaintiffs even $50 when we started this process, there would have been a rebellion in the congregation. We would have quickly been asked to leave. Now, a year and a half later, the idea that came was to offer a grace gift to the people who filed the lawsuit to help them pay their expenses. As I saw the picture of what we were to do, I realized that only a grace gift would work. This church had lost its understanding of grace because of the bitterness that had defiled it. The Plaintiffs did not deserve the $75,000 they wanted in order to settle the lawsuit nor had they earned the right to have these expenses covered. We did not earn or deserve our salvation, but through grace we were saved. My appeal to the church was to offer a grace gift of $50,000 from the church to the plaintiffs. We also asked the General Assembly of Florida to help with an additional $25,000 loan. This put an offer of $75,000 on the table to settle the lawsuit. In a specially called Business Meeting, this proposal was made. What was overwhelmingly amazing and **a great miracle** was that the church had a nearly unanimous vote to try to settle the lawsuit as suggested.

Only a few people voted against the proposal. This is what happens when Jesus shows up. The intercessors prayed, the people listened to God, and the lawsuit was settled.

Obviously, all the hurt and pain did not go away overnight. However, Kendall started having fun and laughing again. Optimism started to capture the hearts of the people and the Pulpit Committee was finally able to do its work. I had worked with the Pulpit Committee for over a year. It was a unified and excited group that took its calling very seriously. The end of the process was a unanimous vote for the new Senior Pastor, an obvious answer to our prayers. We had asked God to call someone with a passion for Kendall. When this pastor and his wife heard of Kendall's interest in their ministry, they began interceding for the church. They found some layouts of the church facility, laid them out on the floor of their home in Illinois, and paced back and forth as they prayed over the church. This new pastor was called by the church. He arrived, and we were moved to another church house. This gave me a quiet place to recuperate from pacemaker surgery. We were so glad to have someone to take over the leadership of Kendall! We were finally free to go home.

It would be nice to say that everything went God's way after the lawsuit was settled. The pain of the division and strife caused many people who filed the lawsuit to leave the church. The new pastor lasted less than two years. In my mind, the reason for his leaving was due to the fact that the church had not yet learned to trust a pastor or to follow his or her leadership. It is a challenge for all in leadership to recognize that our integrity or lack of integrity can have a huge impact on the local body of Christ for many years. Kendall has had several pastors who failed the integrity test, causing great mistrust of leadership. Judy and I were able to earn some of this trust back in the 20 months we served the body, but we know trust doesn't happen overnight. Polarization started around the new pastor who was trying to bring changes to the church. Some were willing to follow, others weren't. Maybe some people felt that he was trying to bring change too quickly in his zeal for the Lord. Maybe some of the changes were not wise for Kendall. However, I believe he and his wife had a great heart for Kendall and can stand before the Lord knowing they were faithful to His call. I am deeply sorry for the pain they experienced.

Praise God, He is not done with Kendall Church. God assured me of this one Sunday morning when we had a very special service. We invited our whole congregation to "Jericho march" seven times around the outside of our church. At the end of the march, the *shofar* (ram's horn) was blown. This was the moment that we asked God to tear down any walls that hindered Christ's work in Kendall. Like Jericho of old, we felt that God wanted us to tear down all of Satan's strategies to try to destroy the church. As a congregation, we prayed to rededicate the Kendall Community Church as a light in the community. We prayed in Jesus' name. We prayed in the power of the blood of Jesus. We prayed urgently and passionately. We asked Jesus to take control. This is how I know Jesus is not done with Kendall Community Church.

We will always carry the people of Kendall in our hearts. Their prayers have continued for us and ours for them. The vote to settle the lawsuit is a great example of what can happen in the most desperate circumstances when Jesus gets His way.

I recently had a conversation with a youth leader in the church who reported that there is more unity in the church today than he has ever experienced at Kendall. God has honored our prayers and when Jesus shows up everything is different!

*"Now to him who is able to do immeasurably more than all we
ask or imagine, according to his power
that is at work within us." Ephesians 3:20*

Chapter 14

Confessions of a Prayer Junkie

Personal Prayer Journey

I am so thankful that Judy and I came to Christ in a Lay Institute for Evangelism, sponsored by Campus Crusade for Christ. We were very blessed that our mentors were some of the staff members who knew how to trust God to do the impossible. Dr. Bill Bright, the founder of Campus Crusade, was an incredible man of faith. Because we saw his deep, abiding faith modeled so well before us, we caught this same faith "bug." We started our Christian life expecting God to move and carry out His promises. All believers attending the Lay Institute for Evangelism in 1971 were challenged to pledge our lives to achieve the Great Commission by the year 2000. They taught us that the Christian life was impossible to live in our own strength. We needed to learn to allow Jesus' resurrection power to live in us. The same power that raised Christ from the dead would come to us as we prayed!

Prayer Models

Throughout my entire ministry, I have tried to find people who really knew how to pray so that I could pray with them. I traveled some with Rev. Ray Bringham who began a prayer ministry called the National Prayer Summit. I volunteered to be on his Board of Directors just to spend time with him. Ray lived an exciting life. Even in his eighties, he still traveled around the world, praying for popes, presidents and anyone else he could engage in prayer. Ray led people to Christ wherever he went. When Ray prayed, revival followed. Because of this, I invited him to come and speak at our newly planted Sawgrass Community Church. His topic was marital fidelity and intimacy. At the end of his message, he challenged married couples to come to an open microphone and repent before the whole church for the times that they had not acted in a Christ-like manner to their mate. Our new church was not used to many traditional kinds of altar calls, and we had never asked for public confessions with an open microphone. Initially, I thought that if even just one couple came forward, I would be surprised. Not one couple came forward to confess and repent of their sins before the congregation; instead, 25 couples came! It was a great day of revival for our church.

God brought several people into my life that He used to teach me about prayer. One of the first was Margaret Kickasola, a powerful intercessor from Lake Wales, Florida. Margaret and her husband, George, lived in a mobile home; their walls were papered with prayer requests from all over the world. They would spend hours walking back and forth, praying for these requests. Miracles followed George wherever he ministered. He was not a speaker, but a behind-the-scenes prayer warrior who would leave healing, deliverance and salvation footprints wherever he ministered. Margaret became an intercessor for me personally for many years. I would call her every time I traveled and would give her my preaching schedule. She was always faithful to pray, and I knew that her prayers were helping to bring God's anointing that was so greatly needed.

Ruth Shinness wrote some incredible books on prayer such as "Unlocking the Heavens." She had a wonderful down to earth way of embracing the supernatural. We prayed together several times at the North American Conference of the Church of God, and each time my faith increased, and my praying became more childlike. She was also a prayer partner for several of my trips to India.

Bill Hilbrick was another man sent from God to teach me how to pray during my years in Dallas. He wandered into my office one day and introduced himself. He had been a Church of Christ pastor for many years. He came to realize that the Holy Spirit was not a living entity to many people in the Church of Christ. Because he was hungering and thirsting for more of the Lord, he was taking classes at Christ for the Nations in Dallas. As he was getting ready to leave my office, he asked if he could pray for me. His intimacy with God and the power of his prayers still touch me when I think of them today. He became a part our church staff on a part-time basis, and we spent about two years together until he moved out of the Dallas area.

David Bryant's Concerts of Prayer and Dick Eastman's Change the World School of Prayer were also very helpful. My library kept growing and contained more books on prayer than on any other topic. I read most of the books written by C. Peter Wagner on spiritual warfare. That led me to attend Fuller Seminary where I could study and pray with Peter himself.

After all these years, I still have a desire to grow in prayer and in intimacy with Jesus. Praying is an intimate relationship with God. There is a secret place in our hearts which, when joined to God, the supernatural moves through us to others. It is the connection between Heaven and earth that Jesus taught us to pray for in the Lord's Prayer. In Matthew 6:10 Jesus said, "Your Kingdom come, your will be done on earth as it is in Heaven." It is the special intimate connection with Jesus and the Father that the Holy Spirit brings into our lives. Heaven comes to earth as we pray, and great battles are won in the world of the Spirit. These wonderful prayer warriors I met had found this place of intimacy and victory in Christ. People who pray want others to enter into the joy and peace of the presence of the Holy Spirit. God trains us to walk in faith as we learn to trust him step by step.

Help for a New Believer

Once while I was still a new believer, I was on my way to teach a Bible study. I went out to start my car and found that the battery was dead. The green light on top of the battery was not shining. I remember laying hands on the battery and praying for its healing. I was startled when the light started shining and I was able to start my car and drive away. In the spirit of transparency, I must admit, that I have since tried this without success!

Another time, I had misplaced my class notes for a lecture I was to give on evangelistic Bible studies. After more than an hour of searching, desperation set in. As I prayed, I reminded the Lord (as if I needed to) that this was His ministry and I needed His help. Immediately, I felt led to go to the side of the garage we rarely frequented. A barrel was sitting against the side of the garage with old newspapers on top of it. Lifting these old papers up, I found my teaching notes. We could never figure out how my notes ended up on that barrel. To God be the glory!

These kinds of experiences have continued over my lifetime of following Jesus. Has God always answered our prayers the way we wanted? No, but I am so thankful that He loves me enough to say "No" or "Wait" at times. He is sovereign, and I am not. Experiencing the freshness of the wind of God through prayer is very addictive. To this day, I have never "arrived" in my prayer life. It has always been a work in progress. However, I have tasted that the Lord is good, and my appetite is growing!

Some amazing God-sightings came during our many years of ministry. I am convinced that nothing of substance happens in the Kingdom of God unless first bathed in prayer. In both the Florida and Oklahoma State Ministries, we started a weekly prayer ministry. We began at the State Office with those pastors and leaders who were within reasonable driving distance. In many ways, I am a weak vessel for the Lord. Do I pray well or long? Probably not. I just know how weak I am without resurrection power. The only way I know how to get resurrection power is to pray.

Cords of Three

Once we had started praying weekly in our State Ministry in Florida, we begin to expand the prayer emphasis by having Cords of Three prayer groups all over the state. "Cords of Three" was a biblical concept of the strength we have together in the Lord. "A cord of three strands is not quickly broken," Ecclesiastes 3:21. Three pastors would commit to get together regularly to pray and encourage one another. I was in a group with Rev. Mike Tobey and Rev. Tony Didway. We experienced great joy as we met together for several years during our prayer commitment.

A strong revival had been going on in Pensacola, Florida for several years. People came from around the world to experience this visitation of the Lord. Mike, Tony and I decided to go see what God was doing. We were enjoying our eight-hour drive together and were sharing what God was doing in our lives. Tony and Mike were starting new churches, and I had recently planted a church, so we had much in common. Mike was reading from the Bible some neat things God had been teaching him about spiritual warfare. I was driving, looking straight down an empty highway. Suddenly a piece of rebar about two feet long flew from the edge of the highway right at the windshield, aimed at my head. There was no explanation for how the rebar flew through the air because there were no other cars or people on the road in front of us at that time. The windshield was totally destroyed. We knew immediately this was the spiritual warfare we had just been talking about. All three of us realized how close we had come to being killed. We went to the next town, got a new windshield and had ourselves a wonderful prayer and praise time together. This is an example of why we need to pray. We felt completely safe in the arms of our Savior and realized that He had protected us from disaster. The revival was refreshing and renewing. It was the first time that I was in a church service where people actually ran to the altar at the end of the service.

Prayer for Warner Southern College

We had been praying much for what was then Warner Southern College, now known as Warner University. We prayed for the instructors, the leadership and the staff, and of course we also prayed for the students. Margaret Kickasola was part of our prayer team and taught us many things about prayer. She had started an on-campus prayer walk each fall. A group of people would walk over the entire campus, praying over each building and for all the new and returning students, professors and administrators. She had committed to pray for Warner Southern for many years and knew about the spiritual battles that were going on at the school. In our prayer time, we were impressed to try to do some hands-on ministry as students arrived for their fall semester. To do this, we started a prayer and worship weekend called a Prayer Summit for all the returning students. Usually from 50 to 100 students would attend, and we would worship and pray in the chapel at the school. The worship would be deep and expressive, and the prayer times were unplanned. Our intent was to really let the Spirit of the Lord lead these meetings. The leadership team included Richard Fields, Mike Sanders, Margaret Kickasola and me. We also asked some off-campus prayer warriors like Ray Bringham to assist us.

When Jesus shows up, supernatural things begin to happen. One Friday evening around midnight, we were praying with about 70 students. I don't know why, but God tends to show up after midnight during prayer meetings. For many years, I have experienced first-hand the movement of God over and among those who seek him urgently. Could it be that around midnight the flesh becomes weaker so the Spirit can work?

All of a sudden, the 70 students who were still praying at midnight went into travail, praying and crying out for lost friends. It sounded like they were crying out from the pit of hell. They were all on the floor in agony for their unsaved friends. The entire leadership team was also face down on the floor. God had shown up!

About this time, one of those unsaved friends had left the school and was driving to a bar in Orlando. Suddenly he knew that he had to turn his car around and come back to the campus. He found our prayer meeting and gave his heart to Christ. His friend had been crying out for him at the altar. This is the power of heart-felt travail. Two of the young people who had been part of our prayer meeting told us on Saturday morning that they had returned home about 2 AM. after our Friday night/early Saturday morning prayer meeting. They tried to go to bed, but they could not sleep. All night they walked through their apartment praying. With no sleep, they showed up for a 9 AM. prayer meeting on Saturday. They did not want to stop praying. Never had they experienced the manifest presence of the Lord like they did on that Friday night and Saturday morning!

There have always been deliverance times that powerfully changed lives, and God really showed

Himself to be strong at these meetings. A girl suffering deep depression was brought to the altar by Margaret Kickasola. She had been in much counseling and medical treatment to no avail. She was the daughter of a pastor, but had such low self-esteem that she could hardly look anyone in the eyes. A group of us started praying for her, and some of the students joined in. The rest sang praise songs as we ministered to her. As we began to pray for her, she became as strong as a weight lifter and tried to break away from those who were praying for her. We asked the Lord to deliver her from the heaviness of depression and to protect her from the enemy. A short time later, with some of the students still praying, she was wonderfully set free. Her body relaxed as she sank to the floor with the reality of Christ's presence all over her. Her countenance and her posture changed, and her eyes and smile were radiant. She shared her testimony of deliverance many times after this meeting and was a powerful and exuberant witness to what God had done. Later, the Lord led her into missions. The last I heard, she was ministering in a communist country.

Another girl shared publically, for the first time, that she had been raped when she was in high school. She had incredible hatred for the rapist, but had kept it all hidden because that event had devastated her and caused false shame and much pain. On this night, with prayer and worship bringing her near the heart of God, she experienced a wonderful deliverance from the darkness surrounding this horrible event and glowed with the freedom she was now experiencing. She chose to forgive this man, prayed publically for his salvation and asked God's blessing on his life. Many other girls who had been abused came and asked her to pray for them. She also went to several churches in the state to testify of the Lord's deliverance. When Jesus shows up, there is so much love and compassion that it is impossible for the enemy to continue to hold people in prison.

The Tennessee Church of God Ministers Meeting

I have had the privilege of preaching at many different venues, and our prayer team would pray faithfully for these meetings. One such meeting was the Tennessee Ministers of the Church of God, a two-day meeting with communion during the last service. As I was in a side room preparing for this service, my heart was disquieted by a thought about communion. Communion had become somewhat rote to me and I wasn't comfortable with my attitude about it. Jesus had given us a mandate to share the bread and cup when we came together so it must be important. I remember crying out to God and asking Him to show all of us that day how we should relate to the Lord's Supper. I decided to take a faith step and told the nearly 100 ministers at the meeting that I felt God was going to show us something special about communion that day. I shared with them my own tepid excitement about communion. I did not feel overly inspired but did have a growing expectancy that God would do something. When the elements for communion were passed, we all met at the altar and the first rows of the church. I read Scripture before taking the bread together. When the first piece of bread touched a pastor's mouth, Jesus showed up. There were hardly any dry eyes as most pastors wept openly. People were confessing sin and bringing it to the blood of Christ. People were on their faces everywhere; no one wanted to leave. Time stood still. Many people missed flights. Christ showed us this great truth about communion: He is at the table with us!

Years later, the State Pastor of the Church of God in Tennessee, J. Morgan Davis, told me that that meeting was one of the greatest events of his life. He mentioned that many of the pastors' lives were changed by Jesus' visitation. When Jesus shows up, He changes everything!

Sawgrass Prayer Teams

Sawgrass Community Church had been birthed by the prayers of 100 prayer partners who continuously took us to the throne of grace. During the fifth year of this church plant, we were stalled as a congregation, unable to break the 200-person barrier. We didn't have a logical answer for this. Some of us decided to go on a juice fast. I made a commitment to a 40-day fast, and many others fasted for lesser times. As we fasted and prayed, God gave an increase. Without doing anything differently, the congregation grew right through the 200-person barrier and we sensed a great anointing on our services.

During the time of fasting, one of our weekly prayer thrusts was for families in our church. Two marriages in our church were failing and another had already failed. We lifted these up almost daily. In one marriage, the mother had left her husband and her four girls about a year earlier and moved to New York City. They were all devastated. Nothing the husband tried to do changed the situation. As we continued to fast, faith became sight. We just knew when we prayed that God was going to move. Shortly thereafter, the estranged husband received a call from a repentant wife, asking if she could come home and work at building a good marriage.

In the other family, the husband often traveled to South America on business. He became involved with a woman there and was preparing his wife and three daughters for his plan to live with the other woman. We had cried out to the Lord over and over about this in our fast. In one of our Sunday services, I was sitting in the first row of the church, praying for the service. I was shocked when this man asked me if he could give a testimony. I asked his wife if she approved, and she was very positive. He walked onto the stage with a large bouquet of red roses, got down on his knees and asked for forgiveness from his wife and from each child. He then asked for forgiveness from the entire church and told how he got saved at an Amway meeting in South America. God turned around an impossible situation. The fuel for this fire was our fasting time; the fire was Jesus Himself!

I also want to share a story of another great miracle. This is a story about the marriage of my niece and nephew, Mark and Tracey Russell. I had the privilege to perform the ceremony for Tracey and Mark at a beautiful wedding venue in Miami, Florida while we were still at Sawgrass. Later, the story concluded after I had become State Coordinator of the Church of God in Florida. What Tracey didn't know when she married Mark, was that he was unfaithful to her during their engagement and right up to the time of the wedding. On the honeymoon, all kinds of guilt and fear caused Mark to totally reject Tracey. She came home from the honeymoon shattered. Over time, the facts of Mark's unfaithfulness came to light, and Tracey's family were deeply angered by his lifestyle. Tracey decided to divorce Mark after a couple years of trying to make it work, and all the family applauded her. Tracey was very angry and deeply hurt by what Mark had done. Some people at Sawgrass encouraged Tracey to trust in the Lord to provide her needs and were praying for a miracle with her marriage. I was one of these, as I felt badly that I had done their marriage counseling and had not uncovered any of the unfaithfulness. I had believed that Mark and Tracey were ideal for one another. Mark knew how to answer questions without revealing his true heart condition. After all, he grew up in the church; surely this made him a Christian.

Mark had developed some friendships with two men who were now involved in the Promise Keepers ministry. They invited him to a Bible study with several other men and began to talk to him about the Lord. They took him to a Promise Keepers event in Washington D.C., and during this meeting, Mark gave his heart to Jesus. He called me and wanted to talk. He wanted to figure out how to put his marriage back together. I cautioned him to put his own life together first and not put pressure on Tracey. Any suggestion of reconciliation mentioned by Tracey brought the wrath of the family down on her. If Mark would have shown up at Tracey's father's house, it would not have been a pretty scene. When Tracey divorced Mark, they already had a small child. Mark had a picture of Tracey and Chase in his wallet. Tracey had told Mark that she wanted the picture back because he obviously didn't care about her or his son. However, he refused to give it up; he kept the picture.

Part of the program at the Promise Keepers event was to ask all the men remove a picture of their family from their wallet and spend time praying over their spouse and children. Mark really had a breakthrough when he joined this prayer. He was broken over his sin and wanted nothing but God's will. He had been telling Tracey that God was changing him and had confessed his wrong-doing to her, but she was too hurt to quickly jump back into the relationship. At the same time that Mark was in Washington, D.C., praying for his family, Tracey was in her car tuning to various radio stations, and came to one that was broadcasting from the Promise Keepers event in Washington, D.C. She heard the directions to pray for the families and envisioned Mark praying for her, using the picture she had wanted to take from him. She pulled her car off the road and through her tears, told God she was frightened by what could transpire if she went back to Mark. In that special moment she also said, "yet not my will but yours be done!" (Luke 22:42b)

Over a period of time, Mark just served Tracey. He got on his knees and asked her forgiveness. They stayed focused on Christ. They started dating again, and I had the joy of marrying them a second time. They have now become a powerful witness for the Lord, telling people what God did for them and can do for others. God has given Tracey a wonderful ministry to women through conferences and published articles in Christian magazines. Mark is a godly leader of his family and has helped lead a church ministry called Celebrate Recovery. They now have three boys and one girl and are serving the Lord with joy. Many of the deep hurts have been healed by the Lord.

God promises us the very fullness of Christ in our lives. He promises that Living Water will flow and quench our deepest thirst when Jesus lives in us. He also promises that our spiritual hunger will be satisfied by the Bread of Life, another name for Jesus. He offers us all of this, but we must reach out for His blessing. The blessing comes when Jesus shows up. We can then give the blessing away to others as Mark and Tracey have done.

"To him who is able to keep you from falling and to present you before his glorious presence without fault and with great joy." Jude 24

Chapter 15
A God-Sized Vision

Chapter 11 told the story of the planting of Sawgrass Community Church. Judy and I were enjoying the ministry in Ft. Lauderdale and I felt this would be my calling for the rest of my life. However, when Jesus shows up, things can change dramatically! Even the thought of saying good-bye to our church family brought tears to our eyes.

In the spring of 1995, I became aware that the General Assembly of the Church of God in Florida was searching for a new State Pastor. This new pastor would help coordinate the various ministries effecting the 125 Church of God congregations in Florida. He would help current churches become healthier and facilitate the planting of new churches. Several pastors asked me to put my résumé into the application process so I prayed and gave some thought to it. I told the Lord that if He wanted me to do that, He would have to make it super clear, like writing it on the wall. I did feel somewhat conflicted because, even though it was not a position I sought, several of my peers told me that I needed to minister to more than one church. My major gifts were encouragement, faith and pastoring, and my ministry and life experiences had given me a heart for pastors who experience many kinds of struggles. I had a growing burden to encourage pastors and help them live out their God-given dreams. I also had a missionary burden and evangelistic passion.

The deadline for submitting résumés came and went and I didn't apply. I heard through the grapevine that a State Pastor had been selected and would soon be introduced. The committee decided to have a one-week fast, and when the committee reconvened, three of the five members of the Search Committee had a sense that they needed to contact me, even though I had not submitted a résumé. They polled the entire committee, and the decision was unanimous to interview me. When Dr. Wiens shared this story with me, I remember hearing a loud, "Oh No!" coming from my lips. Judy heard this and thought that a tragedy had occurred. That groan was my initial reaction to the pain that Judy and I knew we would both experience if we were to leave Sawgrass Community Church. However, we both felt that God had made his will very clear and had indeed "written it on the wall." We immediately began grieving. We did not want to leave all the dear people at the church, yet we could see what God was doing.

After interviewing with the Search Committee, we all had a sense that this was God's plan. God immediately started giving me a vision for the State Ministry. This chapter is part of that early vision. This new challenge launched a new direction for my ministry, one that would be my path for the following 10 years, seven years as State Pastor in Florida and three years as State Minister in Oklahoma.

Looking back, I see this time as a season when God taught me much about leadership. I completed a Doctor of Ministry degree from Fuller Theological Seminary and served 10 years as Chairman of the Publication Board of the Church of God. During this time frame, I was also teaching a course on pastoral leadership as adjunct professor at both Mid-America Christian University and Warner University. I was deeply honored when Warner University awarded me an honorary Doctor of Theology degree.

The part of the new calling that I loved was that nearly every Sunday I was preaching in a different church in Florida and later in Oklahoma. Many people accepted the Lord in these meetings because the local pastors had really prepared people's hearts for the gospel. What an explosion of joy when someone is saved! It is celebrated on earth and in Heaven!

A Great Surfing Story

During this time of serving the churches, I had a very unique experience. My friend Reverend Mike Tobey asked me to preach and hold a leadership conference at Rock Church in West Palm Beach, Florida. First, I was to meet with the leaders on Saturday because they had many questions. I was very surprised that this church had a leadership team that was composed primarily of young adults in their 20's and early 30's. Pastor Mike had done a great job winning and discipling many of these young adults. Their questions were all about how they could be more effective witnesses for Christ to the surfing community. It was an amazing meeting—they could hardly wait for the meeting to end so they could take some of their new ideas to the beach!

We then gathered for worship on Sunday morning. Just before the call to worship, a young man told everyone what the surf reports were for the day. This was a first for me. I had never heard the surf discussed in a church before. This identity with the surfing community was one reason this church was growing so rapidly.

The young people who came were extremely attentive all the way through to the very end of my message. I felt strongly led to remind them that every time someone accepts Jesus, there is a big party in Heaven. When I gave people an opportunity to accept Christ, a young man came to the altar and eagerly accepted the Lord. I later discovered that the young leaders of the church who had been out witnessing on the beach had shared Jesus with him the day before. He did not pray for salvation, but he did promise to come to church. Upon leaving, they told him that when he did accept Jesus, there would be a big party in Heaven to celebrate his decision. When he heard my comment again about a party in Heaven, something clicked in his mind and touched his heart. He was wonderfully saved. The reality of Jesus was so heavy on him, he wouldn't leave the altar. We asked him to go to lunch with us, but he wouldn't leave. We left for lunch, and when we came back an hour and a half later, he was still at the altar. After this young man responded to the altar call, a young lady who was a national surfing champion, came forward and gave her heart to Christ. She too was transformed before our eyes. It was so much fun to be there when Jesus showed up!

Leadership Strategy of Florida General Assembly of the Church of God

As a vision was clarified and processed by leadership and staff, the following objectives became clear:

Objective #1

Church leaders needed to be mentored, encouraged and trained in order to assure the ongoing health and vitality of our current and future pastors and churches. The Mentoring Institute in Florida was birthed to fill this need. It became our leadership development program and it produced good fruit. For many pastors and lay leaders, this was a great encouragement and help. The instructors were godly role models from Warner Southern College as well as from our State Office. They taught and modeled Jesus' lifestyle of deep, caring relationships. This practical training helped pastors learn how to mentor younger pastors.

My doctoral thesis at Fuller Seminary was "A Model for Mentoring Persons Called to Ministry in the Church of God, Anderson, Indiana, in Florida." The Mentoring Institute became a good laboratory to test some of the assumptions in my study. One of these assumptions was that pastors are a lonely group. The Institute validated that having a mentor really met the need for in depth relationships and prevented loneliness. Although we know our Lord has said in Joshua 1:5 NIV, "I will never leave you nor forsake you," he made us for community. We are to come alongside each other to love, help and encourage.

One important move was to bring Greg Wiens on our staff as Florida State Church Planter. Greg and I had many divine appointments over the years, as God brought us across one another's path. Greg is a great leader of leaders and I knew he could do a wonderful job leading the Church of God state ministries. He followed me as State Minister until he started a ministry called Healthy Growing Churches that reaches far beyond the Church of God.

Objective #2

The racial divide that had caused much disunity and separation of the races in our Church of God movement needed to be broken down. One of the cardinal values in the Church of God is the unity of all believers, but we have not always lived this out. I have always had a deep desire to see racial reconciliation because I grew up in a family that had many uncles and a grandfather who were very bigoted. I often heard the "N" word and never heard a positive comment about black people. My parents were not this way, but most of our family was effected by my grandfather's bigotry. For some reason, as a small boy, I began to hate this racism. My grandfather had been a member of the Ku Klux Klan and hated everyone who wasn't like him. I rebelled against this and always tried to find a black friend so I could spite my grandfather. In doing so, I developed some great friendships. I led my grandfather to Christ before he died. He finally realized that Jesus could forgive even his horrible sins.

I was very sympathetic to Martin Luther King and the Civil Rights Movement. It seems that every movie that I have ever seen that focused on slavery or freedom for blacks has brought tears to my eyes. As a white American male, I will never fully know what it feels like to be in a minority, but as I hear the stories of my black brothers and sisters, I am deeply moved with compassion.

There were two General Assemblies in the Church of God in Florida. One was primarily Anglo with a few Hispanics called the General Assembly of the Church of God. The other was predominantly African-American and called the Florida Association of the Church of God. There were two Credentials Committees who had the oversight for ordaining their new pastors. There were two Pastor's Fellowships. At times we would visit back and forth, but basically we were separated.

I knew in my spirit that this division broke the heart of God. One of our key African-American leaders, Pastor James Eubanks, had a dream about the sinfulness of our division and became a great ally in our move to unify the State Ministry. Dr. Melvin James was also a great help. He was a leader in the Florida Association and shared our burden for unity. The decision to invite Dr. Curtice DeYoung to come to Florida proved to be a wise one. An author and consultant on racial reconciliation, Dr. DeYoung helped us understand the issues we were facing. He was Anglo and his wife was African-American so he knew personally the depth of the racial issues.

Three ideas emerged out of this meeting that helped us chart a path toward reconciliation. One was the realization that whatever we did would have to be done around a table of equality, not in majority/minority contexts. Secondly, we learned that reconciliation is not a structural matter, but a heart issue. Thirdly, we needed to take the time to build trust in the process of joining our Credential Committees, our Ministerial Associations, and the General Assembly.

The meeting with Curtice started us on the path of beginning to listen to each other's stories. These were not warm, fuzzy, feel good moments. Some stories were extremely hard to tell and carried great emotion. Some stories were very hard to listen to because they challenged our ways of thinking and our underlying prejudices. There were a small number of Anglos who wanted to move immediately into structure change without the pain of the stories, but we felt the heart issues were really the keys to unity. We felt our African-American friends needed to set the time table for moving forward.

One story in particular touched us all. A black pastor had just been called to a new church assignment. His wife needed to find a doctor near their new home. When she heard of a new doctor who was just starting his practice, she called for an appointment. She was an articulate speaker and her phone voice gave no indication of her race. She was warmly welcomed and sent a packet of information to complete before her first appointment. She was also told that she was one of the first patients for the new doctor. When she arrived at her appointment, the receptionist saw that she was black and apologized, saying that they had made an error. The doctor could not accept any new patients. He was suddenly filled to capacity. This was the "warm welcome" the pastor's wife received to her new community.

The following proposal, known as The 34th St. Covenant, was the agreement worked out by our leaders to outline some steps to reconciliation. It was given to both the Florida General Assembly and the Florida Association for approval.

The 34th Street Covenant

> Whereas, we are committed to be a unified body in the Church of God, and
>
> Whereas, we have been sinfully and tragically divided into the Florida Association and the Florida General Assembly and
>
> Whereas, leaders of both groups have committed to The 34th Street Covenant, and
>
> Whereas we also support the move to one Credentials Committee and a joint Youth Convention in 1997, and
>
> Whereas we also support the plan to have a joint Ministerial Meeting April 7 and 8, 1997 at a site to be announced,
>
> Therefore, we stand in support of The 34th Street Covenant.

Both Assemblies unanimously supported the proposal, and we took the process one step at a time. The Credentials Team leaders met and carefully crafted a new set of bylaws that brought both groups together. The new group included three African-Americans, one Hispanic and three Anglos. Our Ministerial Fellowship leaders came around the table and drafted a new structure for one Ministerial Fellowship. The General

Assembly would require more time and would come together after I left my ministry in Florida.

To accomplish the joining of the General Assemblies, we had to deal with a concern of our black brothers and sisters. Our Florida State Office was in Lake Wales, a town that had once been a Ku Klux Klan stronghold. At one point, the Grand Dragon of the Klan had made his home in Lake Wales. We did not realize it, but when our black brothers and sisters came to Lake Wales, they felt a distinct discomfort and fear. I think they were spiritually sensitive to the evil that was still resident around them. Unknown to us, they were not always treated well in local restaurants and area businesses.

Dr. Greg Wiens proposed that if the building location was hindering reconciliation, then the building should be sold. This was a relatively new, state-of-the-art building for State Ministry. However, the reconciliation process was too important to let anything hinder it. The building was sold to Warner University and the State Office was moved to Orlando. The final step was to become one General Assembly. What a wonderful picture of unity in diversity! We celebrate diversity with meetings among Hispanics and blacks, but we can now experience the one church for which Christ died.

Objective #3

Dr. Mike Sanders, Campus Pastor at Warner University, had a dream to raise up youth leaders in our congregations who would be well-trained to be the next generation of leaders in the Church of God movement. Mike had a vision to help high school young people understand their calling and vocational direction in light of a Christian world view. He felt our state ministry could work with local churches to identify, train and encourage young people who had a call on their lives. He had shared this idea with others, but his dream had not been realized. Together, by the grace of God, we made plans to carry out Mike's dream.

We felt that annual discipleship training/mentoring seminars for young people who were showing leadership potential in their local churches would be very beneficial. This was a partnership between Warner University and the Church of God in Florida. We surveyed these young people and discovered that they desperately wanted godly mentors to speak into their lives. We began to work with the local churches in order to develop these young leaders and to help them define their life-calling and direction. We wanted the local churches to celebrate these young leaders and involve them in their ministries. This endeavor was very fruitful and grew greatly from year to year. It became a model for the whole country and today many states as well as our National Church of God Youth Leadership Team are speaking into the lives of young leaders. Mike was faithful to the vision God gave him, and Jesus showed up to bring much fruit through this effort. The lives of many young people were revolutionized through these training seminars. Many of these students continued preparing for ministry at Warner University in Lake Wales.

Objective #4

Believing that Jesus modeled coaching as an important part of His lifestyle, we wanted to launch a coaching movement for leaders and pastors to train them to effectively coach others. Coaching is different than mentoring. A coach asks questions that produce self discovery; a mentor guides a less experienced person by building trust and modeling positive behaviors. While in the position of State Pastor of the General Assembly of the Church of God in Oklahoma, I received an invitation to attend a Coaching Conference directed by Bob Logan. Bob is the author of the book *Coaching 101* and had developed a powerful coaching website, www.Coachnet.org. This was more than a conference because each person attending had a coach, certified by Bob Logan, who would coach each attendee for six months. Attendees were also to develop a relationship with someone they could coach. This would be monitored by his or her coach. It was an expensive process, costing several thousand dollars and requiring six months to complete the training and certification.

Because I was enthralled by the way Jesus coached leaders, the possibility of this training increased my desire to attend. However, I shoved the registration into my desk drawer and forgot about it. For some reason, I just could not throw it out, and one day it reemerged from my desk drawer. This time there was an overwhelming feeling that I needed to go to this training. Judy and I bit the bullet to pay for it. I went to California and had no idea how God would use this training. Because of this training God redirected our steps for several years. Kermit Wilson, a Church of God State Pastor from California, also attended this training. Kermit and I were later certified as Coaches through Coachnet. What we learned about coaching helped us understand how to come alongside and help other people accomplish their God-given dreams. Good questions from a coach can help people know how they can overcome obstacles that hinder the achievement of their dreams. Ways of overcoming these obstacles are often residing inside of the person we coach. The key is for an effective coach to ask powerful questions that will help draw those answers out.

Shortly after my certification by Bob Logan, Rev. John Newton called me. John was coordinating Church Planting and Church Health at the national level for the Church of God. He wanted to establish a program to train coaches across the Church of God. He had already had conversations with Bob Logan about a partnership between our organizations, and Kermit Wilson and I were involved in those conversations. We were asked to train about 20 coaches each in order to officially start this coaching movement and include proper certification through Coachnet. Thus, the Coach Training Initiative (CTI) was born and became a powerful life-changing ministry. In the following six years that this training was held around the country, 250 Church of God leaders and many of our State Pastors across the country were trained and certified through a hands-on coaching experience.

Our Leadership Team was led by Rev. John Newton. Rev. Mike Claypool, Rev. Ken Wiedrick, Rev. David Wynn, Rev. Kermit Wilson and myself rounded out the Leadership Team. We were all excited to see how God would move in this ministry. We had many testimonies regarding the transformation of churches, families and pastors through this training.

My personal involvement in coaching led to coaching clusters in Church of God congregations in Arkansas, Missouri, Iowa, Illinois, Oklahoma and Florida, and with Mike Claypool in North Carolina and Ohio. Nearly 50 churches in these clusters committed to a one-year process of coaching. The State Ministry and the local churches shared the cost. Two general meetings were held about 12 months apart, and I coached the pastors one-on-one monthly, mostly by phone. Pastors brought key leaders from their churches to the general, one-day meetings. At these working meetings, the church leaders worked on developing and implementing a plan to reach their vision. The pastor would not only be coached, but he or she was also to coach another person in their sphere of influence, so we could monitor them in their coaching development.

I was also a certified consultant for Natural Church Development which provided us with an assessment tool to measure eight health parameters of the churches. It featured a survey that would be filled out by about 30 church members. The premise was that just as healthy vines and plants grow, so healthy churches will grow as well. This tool was helpful in showing strengths and weaknesses of the churches and where to spend prayer time and energy to help it become healthier.

As a result, many churches and pastors became more focused on their mission and were greatly encouraged. Jesus was the best coach who ever lived. When we encountered Him in this coaching movement, we all sensed we were along for a supernatural ride.

"But you will receive power when the Holy Spirit comes on you, and you will be my witnesses in Jerusalem, and in all Judea and Samaria, and to the ends of the earth." Acts 1:8

Chapter 16

Legacy in India and the World

He showed us his stomach and the large scars where his father's machete had struck him over and over. SA.* told us that the day he was baptized as a Christian, his Hindu dad and brothers tried to kill him. Now he was a pastor who had recently had a very bad stroke. It was very difficult for him to walk and talk. Yet as we left India after our second trip, he was walking from Calcutta to Bhutan to preach the gospel in some places where it had never been preached before. This is the passion that is propelling the gospel in India. I think it would be wise for me to confess that I received much more from our India/Bangladesh/Bhutan/Sri Lanka partners than they received from me. I saw Jesus in them through their willingness to suffer for Him. Rather than shrinking back their suffering energizes them to be more aggressive witnesses.

Stories like this one have changed the lives of many of us who have travelled in the third world. God is moving in miraculous ways in these hard to reach areas. This chapter speaks of Objective #5, which has to do with reaching beyond the USA into the world.

Specifically, it tells the story of the people who have been in partnership with us to get the gospel to N. India, Bangladesh, Bhutan and Sri Lanka. Chapter 15 described the first four objectives of State Ministry in Florida. This chapter covers Objective #5.

Objective #5

We wanted to launch a partnership between churches in Florida and churches and leaders like SA. We focused on some of the most unreached people groups in the world in India and Bangladesh. For some time, I had personally been reading and hearing mission reports regarding how few mission dollars were being spent among the most unreached people in the world, most of whom lived in the 10/40 window. The 10/40 window is the latitude and longitude of the geographical area that encompasses most of Asia. It includes the massive population centers of China and India, and much of the Arab world. In much of this window, little investment of mission dollars had been made because missionaries cannot go to sensitive areas. Obviously, some westerners still find ways to connect with some of these countries, but often under very dangerous circumstances. Like many mission groups, we chose to work with partners in the indigenous church who know the language and the culture of the area.

As our State of Florida prayer team met once a week to pray, a growing burden for these unreached people emerged. One of the people who attended that prayer meeting was Dr. Robert Clark who had worked as a missionary in Bangladesh for 16 years. It also included Rev. Richard Fields who heads a 501(c)(3) missions organization called Helping Hands in Motion (HHIM). As Dr. Clark spoke with the prayer team, he would start shedding tears all over my desk. He would then look at Richard and me and say, "Do you think those of us who have so much could do something for those who have so little?" The three of us gravitated towards one another and we started crying with Dr. Clark regarding the needs of the unreached people in India and Bangladesh. Many times Dr. Clark would tell us stories of his mission among the poorest of the poor in Bangladesh. He lived without running water or electricity in a village that was very poor. He could have lived in a nice mission home, but he chose not to so that he could identify with the people he was trying to reach. He brought the gospel to many places in Bangladesh where most of the people had never heard it.

God really spoke to us through Dr. Clark, and in 1998 we decided to take a fact-finding trip to India and Bangladesh. We invited Global Missions, the outreach arm of the Church of God in Anderson, to partner with us. We were most appreciative that they sent Rev. Mike Kinner with us on most of our early journeys. We recruited seven Florida pastors and one layman to go with us on this eye-witness tour of India and Bangladesh, making a total of 12 men. As we travelled, we asked God to show us potential partners who shared our burden for reaching people in the 10/40 window. We were looking forward to supporting and encouraging the indigenous church in areas of ministry where we shared common goals.

As we prepared to go, Dr. Clark volunteered to be our "on the field" mission's instructor because he knew the language and culture of the people that we would visit. God answered our prayers on that first trip. He led us to national leaders who shared our passion to reach the unreached people in pioneering church planting. In most of these places, the population was less than .1% Christian. The leaders that we chose to partner with are now some of our best friends on earth. We are indebted to Dr. Clark, who has since gone to Heaven, for leaving us his legacy of concern and burden for the lost.

While in India, I had an encounter that would change the rest of my life. As I unpacked my bag after flying and traveling for 35 hours from Florida to Calcutta, I looked out of my hotel window to a great view of the street below. People were milling and moving in a nameless mass up and down the street. Across the street was a Hindu shrine attended by a Hindu priest. He stood in front of the Goddess Cali, the Goddess of Destruction and the namesake of Calcutta. She holds the heads of the people she has decapitated because they didn't worship her. These very poor Indian people would give their few rupees to this priest to appease a goddess who was made of wood and stone. She didn't answer prayers. She didn't help people. She shared no message of love and forgiveness. She was a lifeless wood and stone statue. Her only power comes through the demon spirits who deceive the people through her.

Hindu Shrine

While looking at this frustrating scene, I had a vision of 16,000,000 people in the streets of Calcutta looking at me and asking me, "What are you going to do to help us?" Those myriad numbers of eyes staring at me and asking for deliverance still haunts me.

On that first trip to India, the 12 of us met several leaders whom we felt would be good partners. Because of the sensitive nature of these ministries, I am giving fictitious names to our partners, Rev. Sumar*, Rev. Matthew*, Rev. Bimuh* and Rev. Sahu*. We later met Rev. Thomas* and evangelist William* with whom we developed a partnership in Bangladesh. Lastly, we built a relationship with Pastor Kahwa*. We had the joy of praying for and laying hands on Pastor Kahwa* when he was commissioned and sent out by leaders of the NE Indian church to reach the T* people. We have also partnered with Rev. Bijah* who works among M* people. He is now being used around the world to train other leaders in effective ministry to the M* people.

Since 1998, groups have returned to India almost every year, and mission teams are going several times a year. Some of our pastors have made multiple trips, but we try to recruit new pastors on each trip we take. The ongoing leadership group was truly a partnership. It involved Global Outreach of the Church of God, Helping Hands in Motion, The General Assembly of Florida and J. Boedeker Ministries. I started J. Boedeker Ministries as a 501(C)(3) non-profit ministry because I had many friends who would give to this mission because they knew me. The predominant leadership was initially from Global Outreach, but reassignment of personnel led Rev. Richard Fields, Dr. Clark, Rev. Denny Huebner and me to pick up more responsibility for the N. India and Bangladesh ministry. The following demonstrates the many ways God led us and provided for the ministry through many of His humble servants.

Our first project was to purchase a Discipleship and Worship Center in Calcutta. I remember that as we came back home, all of us were in agreement that the number-one priority was the need in Calcutta. The only church building available to the Calcutta Church of God was a building in the slums with human excrement running from the top floors down the outside of the building to the street. We found a house for sale for $38,000 that had enough space for group worship and enough room for training programs. We simply put a brochure together and mailed it to churches in Florida, asking them to take an Easter offering for this building. We were thrilled that $55,000 was raised. A key in being able to do this was the testimony of the seven pastors and the layperson who had accompanied us on our trip.

Discipleship Center Calcutta

Along with purchasing the building, another high priority was raising support for church planters. We have helped support evangelists in India, Bangladesh, Sikkim, Bhutan and Sri Lanka. These workers are involved with Muslims, Hindus, Buddhists and tribal peoples. We have built many church buildings and multiple structures for children's ministries. Our team has built a four-floor Discipleship Center in Sikkim, purchased property for two future Discipleship Centers and bought a flat in New Calcutta in order to reach Information Technology workers for the Lord. A special thanks to Crossings Community Church for this flat. It is finally producing the fruit that they had expected.

A list of some of our projects to help the indigenous churches reach their God-given vision is as follows: We bought computers, cameras, Proclaimers (solar video systems to show the "JESUS" film), Acclaimers (solar audio systems to play the gospel in various languages), sewing machines, chickens, rickshaws, a refrigerator, automobiles, motorcycles and bicycles for evangelists and church planters.

We have also provided training for pastors and planters, a Discipleship Program for women, a Marriage Retreat, a Parenting Retreat for training Regional Coordinators, and a Trauma Workshop for people who have known tragedy or persecution. Sister D* and Sister A* and their team, known as *Matthew 28:20 Women*, have had a remarkable ministry. They have brought much needed, in-depth teaching and discipleship to people in India and Sri Lanka. This started out as a women's ministry, but the change in the women was so great, the men begged for the training also. This has been a transformational ministry among many leaders in India and Sri Lanka.

We have printed literature, translated many resources in various languages and have done multiple medical camps. Doctors, nurses and helpers from Crossings Community Church have provided wonderful medical services to people with great needs. Many individuals with medical needs have been helped by donors to this ministry. In some cases, they were brought to the states for medical help. In other cases, a second opinion diagnosis was made in the states with follow up being done in India. All in all, churches and individuals have given Helping Hands in Motion and J. Boedeker Ministries well over $1,300,000 since 1998. These dollars represent the hearts and lives of many people who are burdened for the wonderful people living in the 10/40 window. All of these funds went directly to our partners in India. Once again, we realize these funds are a miracle that happens when Jesus shows up. Our initial idea was that maybe we could raise $20,000 to help the ministry in N. India. God had something very different in mind!

None of this would have transpired without the leadership of Rev. Richard and Sister Debi Fields who founded HHIM. They have been a catalyst and major fund-raiser for this entire ministry. Debi and Richard have two of the purest hearts for God of anyone I have met. Both have a burden for our friends and partners in the 10/40 window. Rev. Denny Huebner played a key leadership role on the Board of HHIM. He has led each church that he has pastored to give generously to this ministry. He led the Oak Grove Church in Tampa to purchase materials for 50 buildings for small village churches in India. Richard Fields is a biker, so he has many relationships in the biker community. The Christian Motorcycle Association (CMA) supplied many motorcycles to evangelists in India and Bangladesh. When we first sent Acclaimers and Proclaimers to India and Bangladesh, a number of these were provided free by the manufacturers. They have helped us get the gospel out through the "JESUS" film and through printed scripture into the 10/40 window. We are so thankful for the Lord's provision through these groups.

Major help has come from Spread the Word, the Youth Mission outreach of the Church of God. They have helped in some large projects such as the purchase of several automobiles. The youth of the Church of God in Missouri helped build a church building in Sikkim.

Another important ministry has been a partnership with our national leaders and Compassion International to minister to the needs of poor children. We helped in both Bangladesh and India to establish these ministries by providing facilities, equipment and water. There were nearly 400 children in the program at the Bhutan border and another 350 in the Tea Gardens. Many of these areas have no electricity, and elephants still range through the compound. We have also helped with several more Church of God/Compassion projects in Bangladesh. These poor children became part of an after-school program which offers them academic help, one good meal a day, medical care and spiritual formation. The children are sponsored by donors in America who support them with a monthly gift of $38. The Indian Government has now made it very difficult to get money into India from the United States for anything suspected of having a Christian message. For this reason, the future of this ministry is unknown to us, but not to God. We are trying to keep the program going for the younger children as Helping Hands has raised some funds to keep them involved.

Throughout these years, there have been difficult challenges, but we also have seen so many miracles in this ministry. In 1998, a group of us went to Meghalaya to attend the annual Assembly of the Church of God. Our first meeting was in a large church building where several thousand gathered. As the meeting moved towards the weekend, a golf course was rented to hold the 35,000 expected to attend.

Gathering in Shillong

I was scheduled to be the Sunday morning preacher at the conference. On Friday night, some of the brothers from the church visited our team and wanted us to know that there were some threats. They had heard that government people were scheduled to be in the audience on Sunday to check us out. They conveyed that there might be some danger to us. I quickly volunteered to have one of the Indian pastors replace me so we didn't cause our friends problems. They were not in favor of us doing that. They suggested that I could preach without giving an altar call if that would make me more comfortable. I could tell they did not really want this alternative. Basically, they came to us so they could warn us and call us all to pray so we could hear God's direction. Messages went out, and many people around the world prayed for our safety and that the Lord would show us what to do. We had a great sense of peace and felt we should go ahead with our original plans. There were no incidents in the preaching service and we were all relieved and thankful.

The sermon was almost finished when I had a deep impression that I was to say a word to anyone who had come to observe and report the happenings at this large gathering. I told these people that they were having a divine appointment that day, that God knew they would be at this meeting and that He couldn't wait to share His love with them. I told them if they would have been the only person who attended, God would have come to minister his love to them. I then gave the altar call and invited people to put their trust in Christ. There was a great response; many made their way to a large altar. About 100 workers prayed with people who came forward.

Praying at Altar

When I get to Heaven, I am going to ask the Lord if some of those government people who were a threat to us were saved that morning in Shillong, India.

Another miracle occurred in 2000 when the 10 pastors who traveled with us were asked to sing a special song in the service on Sunday morning. This was totally unplanned, and we weren't singers. The crowd of 35,000 people sang a cappella, and to me it sounded angelic. It was miraculous that we agreed to sing, and it was miraculous that we could find a song that we all knew. However, the real miracle came later. Only about half of us had ever sung in public, but some were loud enough, and a few were good enough to make up for the rest of us. As we sang, photographers were taking many pictures. Part of the interest they had in us was that we looked like giants. Some pastors were 6'8", 6' 4", 6'5" and several others were over 6'2". It was quite a picture for the news service to take in from their 5'8" perspective!

The weekly newspaper that circulated over much of the mountainous area of Meghalaya had a front-page picture and headline, reporting about the meeting and the "famous" American singing group. Inside the paper was a summary of the gospel message. Satan tried to stop the message, but God took the Good News and spread it all across the country! When Jesus shows up there is nothing impossible. We believe that God will bring the continent of Asia to Christ.

Prepare to be amazed when you get in on what God is doing in world missions. We never know when twists and turns in our journey will become a great move of God. Many times it happens when we least expect it.

We met Pastor M* in Sikkim in 1998. The area of Sikkim in the Himalayan Mountains close to China and Nepal. Its a beautiful place and a vacationing mecca for wealthy Indian business people. Pastor M* was introduced to us by Rev. B*, one of the mission leaders of the Meghalaya Church. Sikkim was a Buddhist Kingdom for many years, and subsequently was annexed to India. Most of the people living there were Buddhists, but there were Hindu and Tibetan Buddhist influences, also. Many people in the area speak the Nepali language.

Pastor M* had been a Buddhist monk before his conversion to Christianity. After his conversion, he had a vision for reaching Sikkim as well as Nepali-speaking people in the adjoining countries with the gospel.

When we visited there in 1998, we met the people in the new church that he had planted. There were a total of about 30 people attending. He was already discipling some young men to reach out into other areas of Sikkim. At the time, the population of Sikkim was about 2% Christian and there was much persecution. Even with many governmental restrictions and persecution, the new church was started. Pastor M*, a single man, was raising seven orphans. Because he had faith in Jesus Christ and because he had planted a church, he had been beaten and robbed several times. It was not an easy path for him.

A breakthrough came in the process of planting this church because God had used Pastor M* to raise a man from the dead. After being called by a church family, he was told that a beloved family member had died. When he arrived at the family home, the man had been dead for some time. Pastor M prayed for him and God raised the man to new life. When the man was raised, he said that he had been in Heaven and was told that he was seven days early. Pastor M then led this man to Christ. He died seven days later as a saved, born-again Christian. This miracle got a lot of attention and God used it to produce faith in many people's hearts in that area.

There also was a miracle that involved the small church building used by Pastor M and his small flock. The church building was built on a mountainside; a mudslide had destroyed every other building on the hillside except this one small church. The people could not deny the protection of the Lord and that a miracle had happened.

Pastor M*'s greatest need was for a place to meet for worship and a place to disciple and train people. Land is very expensive in this area of the Himalayas, but we prayed and God brought churches and pastors like Rev. Denny Huebner and Rev. David Walker and many others to help build this center. Rev. Richard Fields, founder of HHIM, was on board to coordinate the effort, and his leadership was critical to the success of this project. Today there is a beautiful church building with a four-story Discipleship Center that has a church of about 300 people meeting in it. The Discipleship Center can hold about 1500 people for special occasions. We should note that Pastor M* also has an association with the church in Meghalaya.

Discipleship Center Sikkim

What has happened in the Kingdom of Sikkim? Pastor M* now has the oversight of 32 churches in Sikkim. He has also expanded into Bhutan which only recently has allowed the gospel. Sikkim has grown from 2% in 1998 to 15% Christian. On one visit, we saw 60 people baptized during one Sunday meeting. Many of these had previously been Buddhists. Muslims are also coming to Christ after seeing visions of Jesus. The T* people are also coming to Christ, even though they might be the most resistant people on the planet. We have welcomed former militant Hindus into God's family. One new church that we visited was started by 14 converted Buddhist families. Even though North India is only .1% Christian, God is moving mightily in the most difficult places. Our God is an amazing God! It has been wonderful to be in the places in the world where God is working, and Jesus is showing up!

The power of God is also visible in Bangladesh. Our team was in a small Muslim village to meet with a group of people who had come to Christ. In this meeting of about 30 people, we were asked to share a greeting, but we were also told there was a Muslim Mullah in attendance. We didn't exactly know the ramification of this so we were very cautious in our comments. Soon a young evangelist addressed the small group. He was a fiery young man who preached Christ with great power. Even though we didn't know the language spoken, we could sense his intent because the Spirit gave witness to us. When this young man finished, the older Mullah was asked to speak. Through our interpreter, we understood that this older Mullah had a vision of Jesus and was affirming everything the young evangelist shared. I took a picture of this Mullah with my camera. In the place where his head should have been, there was a bright, shining light that I believe was the light of Jesus. (Unfortunately, this picture is buried in a computer that crashed). When we went outside, the whole Muslim village had brought all the sick people to be prayed over, and everyone else wanted us to pray a blessing on them. This is what happens in the realm of the supernatural in the Muslim world when Jesus shows up!

This is the last chapter of this book. However, the last chapter of our lives has yet to be experienced. It will be lived out in whatever time Judy and I have left on this earth before we meet our wonderful Savior. It will be lived by our children and our grandchildren. It will be experienced by those we have led to the Lord and discipled. It will be the concluding life chapter for witnesses in India, Sri Lanka, Bhutan and Bangladesh. It will be lived by you who are reading this book. This has been a story about Jesus. When Jesus shows up, incredible things will happen in your life! Speak it, sing it, show it; share it; shout it.

How can we enter into eternal life? What does the Bible say? "The word is near you; it is in your mouth and in your heart," that is, the word of faith we are proclaiming: That if you confess with your mouth, 'Jesus is Lord,' and believe in your heart that God raised him from the dead, you will be saved. For it is with your heart that you believe and are justified, and it is with your mouth that you confess and are saved." Romans 10:8-10. He will make every chapter of our lives abundantly fulfilling as we wait on His return or on Him calling us home.

Amen. Come, Lord Jesus! Revelation 22: 20 b.